S0-BSE-686

One Dog, Two Dogs, Three Dogs, Four...

Twice-Told Tales of Several Dogs Living in a Beach House on the Gulf Coast

Paul Estronza La Violette

With Illustrations by Patricia Rigney

Waveland, Mississippi

One Dog, Two Dogs, Three Dogs, Four…

For reprint information or any business relating to this publication,
Please contact:
laviolette@datasync.com

Published by Annabelle Publishing
Post Office Box 68
Waveland, MS 39576

Annabelle Publishing is a two-person company consisting of Paul and Stella La Violette. Information on the company may be found on the company website: www.annabellepublishing.com

Library of Congress Control Number: 2007903897

ISBN 0-9673936-8-X
EAN 9-780967-3936-8-X

Some of the stories in this book began their lives as Sunday columns in the *Sea Coast Echo,* a regional newspaper in Bay St. Louis, Mississippi. Others are taken from my books, *Views from a Front Porch, Where the Blue Herons Dance,* and *Waiting for the White Pelicans.* They are all true stories and the events described in them happened more or less as described here.

987654321

First Edition

TABLE OF CONTENTS

Other Books by Paul Estronza La Violette by Annabelle Publishing*

Views from a Front Porch,
Waiting for the White Pelicans,
Where the Blue Herons Dance,
Sink or Be Sunk,
Blueberry Peaches, Red Robin Pie (with Stella La Violette),
Holly!!
and
A White Egret in the Shallows

---

* We are self published. Please see our website for information on these books: www.annabellepublishing.com.

THIRTEEN THINGS YOU CAN LEARN FROM YOUR DOG

1. *When your loved one comes home, run to greet him.*
2. *Take naps.*
3. *Eat with gusto.*
4. *When it's hot, drink lots of water. Splash it around when you do. Show you appreciate it.*
5. *Take naps.*
6. *Never bite, growl. If it's a friend, growl silently.*
7. *Give unconditional love. Do this twice each day. Increase this amount on weekends and holidays*
8. *Take naps.*
9. *Stay close to your loved one in times of stress. Get closer when things get worse. Get as close as you can when things get very bad.*
10. *When you want something badly, dig for it. Dig hard. Make loud noises when you dig.*
11. *Take naps.*
12. *If you are happy show it, wag your tail. If you are really happy, wag it harder.*
13. *Take more naps.*

(See page 92)

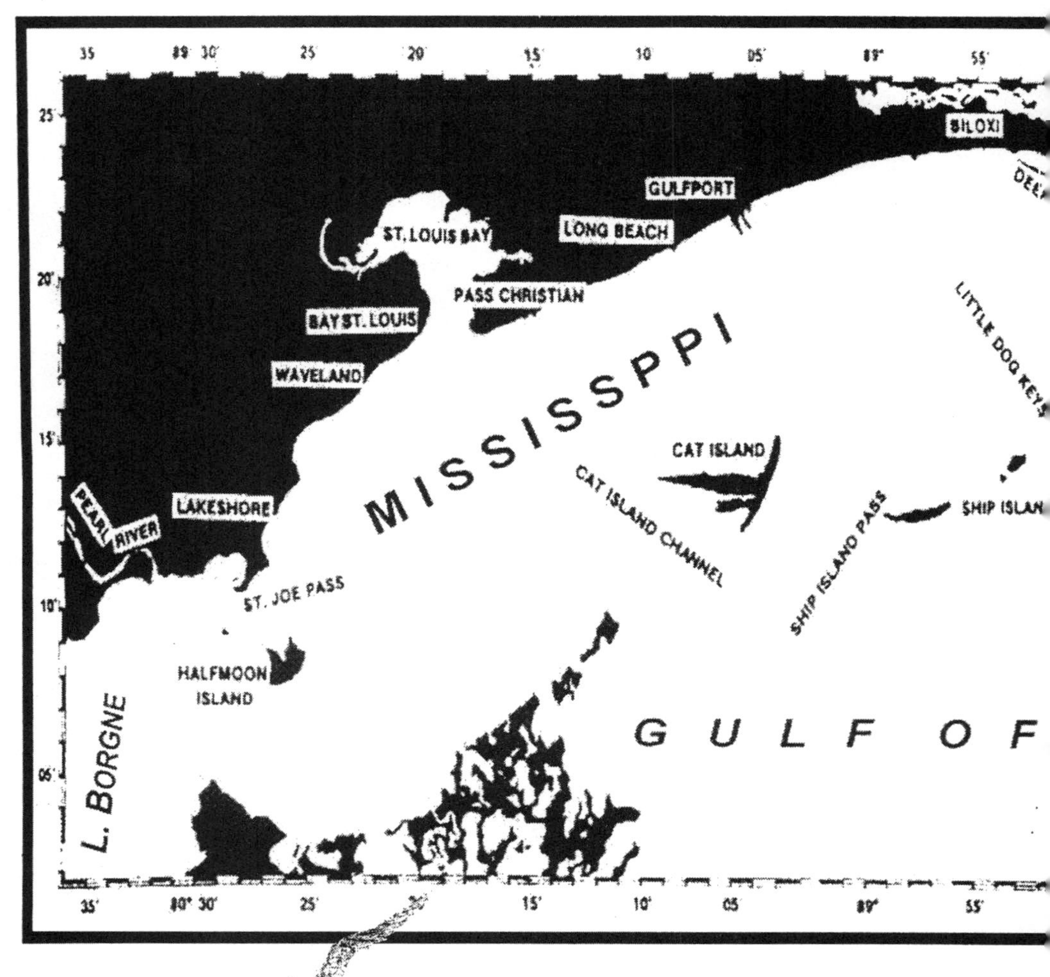
BILOXI
GULFPORT
LONG BEACH
ST. LOUIS BAY
PASS CHRISTIAN
BAY ST. LOUIS
WAVELAND
MISSISSPPI
LITTLE DOG KEYS
CAT ISLAND
CAT ISLAND CHANNEL
SHIP ISLAND PASS
PEARL RIVER
LAKESHORE
ST. JOE PASS
HALFMOON ISLAND
L. BORGNE
GULF OF

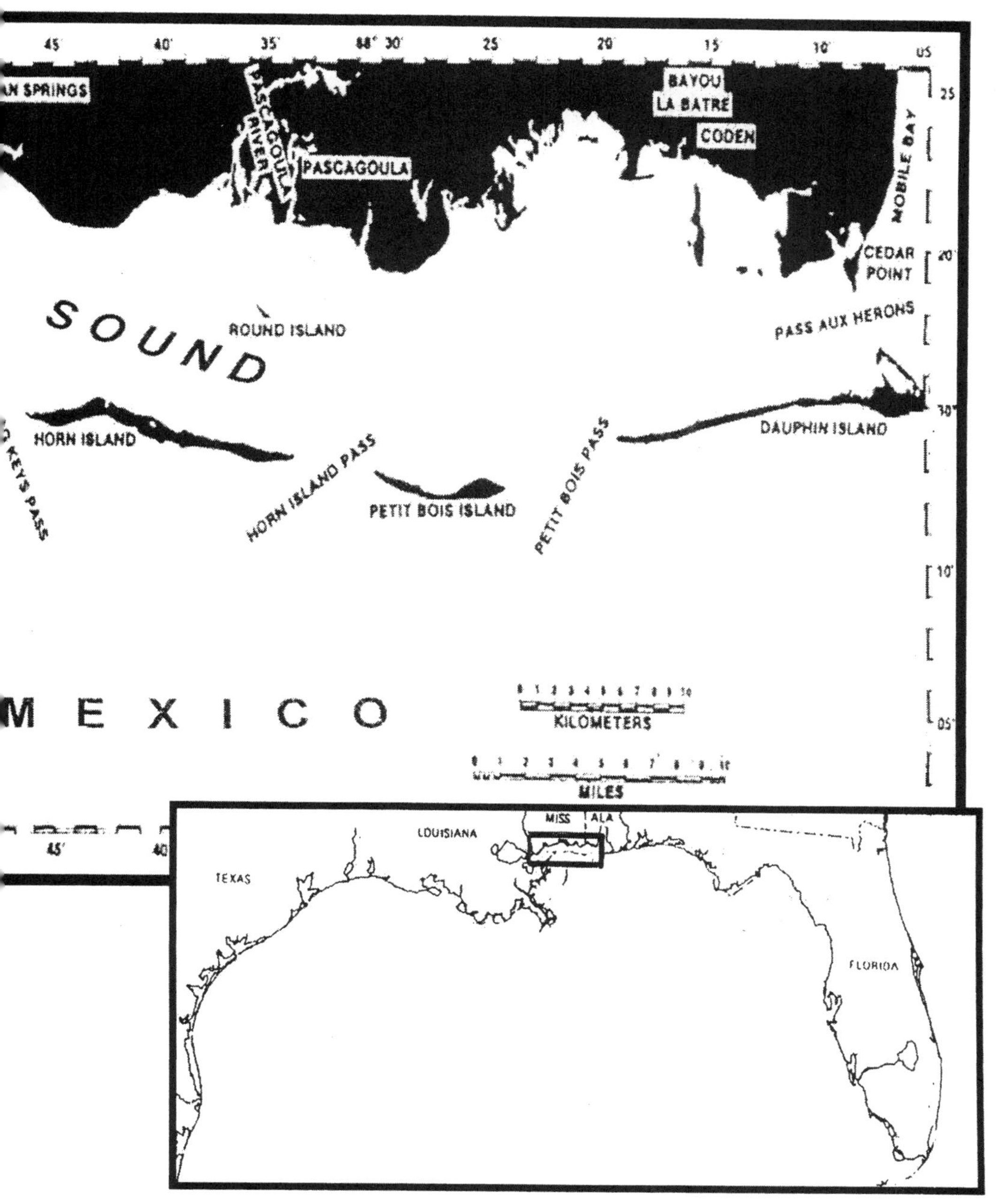

45'
40'
35'
88° 30'
25'
20'
15'
10'
05
AN SPRINGS
PASCAGOULA RIVER
PASCAGOULA
BAYOU LA BATRE
CODEN
MOBILE BAY
25
20'
CEDAR POINT
SOUND
ROUND ISLAND
PASS AUX HERONS
HORN ISLAND
DAUPHIN ISLAND
30'
KEYS PASS
HORN ISLAND PASS
PETIT BOIS ISLAND
PETIT BOIS PASS
10'
MEXICO
KILOMETERS
05'
MILES
LOUISIANA
MISS
ALA
TEXAS
FLORIDA

PREFACE

"You wrote a book about Holly, why don't you write one about Jennie?" This was from my wife, Stella. She had come into the living room and found me sleeping on the floor beside the couch. When I awoke, startled by her entrance, she greeted me with this admonition.

I looked around.

There lying on the floor less than a foot from me was Jennie, our old gray Weimaraner sound asleep, snoring quietly, but managing to stay as close to me as she could. On the other hand, Holly, our black tomcat, was on the other side of the room doing his cat thing, lying in the warm sun near the sliding glass door to the porch, probably wanting to go out.

I sat up, leaned my back against the couch, and looked at the two. She was right, of course. I had written a book about the first four years of my association with Holly. Its title, *Holly!!*, aptly describes those four years. The fact that Holly was across the room, while Jennie was sound asleep beside me during my nap, speaks a lot about the relationship of the three of us.

When I take a nap during the day, I usually take it on the living room floor and Jennie usually joins me, lying close to me and staying there till I wake up. Her doing this is an interesting phenomenon. When we had other dogs, they did this as well. I'll write about this later in this book. But it's Stella's rebuke that I'm addressing here, and it goes a great deal to explaining this book.

Let me set the stage a little. This book covers a period when Stella, Holly, Jenny, and I lived in a small Mississippi town. Our house then was a large sprawling beach house bordering the waters of the Mississippi Sound. It was a tranquil life and one that Stella and I over a period of more than thirty years enjoyed. Part of that enjoyment was because we had the close wonderful company of Jennie and several other dogs that preceded her. There are many ways to spend that many years, but we believe our way was exceptionally nice.

It is this intimate closeness with these dogs that's really my answer to Stella's question. It's a little hard to explain, but let me try.

Look at the frontispiece of this book. The dog pictured is Jennie, but it could be any of the several dogs we have had. In the picture, there is no question of what Jennie is thinking. Clearly written on her face is all the charisma that is her. It shows her demeanor, her spirit, and her willingness to do whatever is asked. It shows exactly what she is: a wonderful, kind, selfless companion that Stella and I treasured and will remember all the years of our lives. All of our several dogs were like that.

Cats are different. The book that I wrote about Holly also pictures him in the frontispiece. The demeanor of the young cat that stares back at you from the page is starkly different from the open, friendly face of Jennie. What you see is an enigma that if viewed at the end of the four-year period covered in the book would still project the same mystique.

The day a friend handed me a cat and, telling me it was a nice cat, walked me out the door of her shop, I found I was the owner of an exotic animal that I knew nothing about. In the years that followed and still today, I have found that my knowledge of cats has not increased one iota.

In effect this was why I wrote *Holly!!* I found that with Holly, I was exploring unknown territory, regions that were blank in my experience, and with the book, I wanted to provide documentation of that experience.

Not so with Jennie. Jennie was a known entity, a familiar being whose presence was part of our everyday life, a being whose thoughts and loves were simple and devoid of the slightest wile. To write about her would be as if I were writing about a good book, a nice meal, or a rather pleasant day. Writing about the everyday intimacies I shared with Jennie would be far different than writing about the exotic antics of Holly.

But reflecting on Stella's comment, I found that in the past several years I had written short stories that included Jennie as well as our other dogs. These stories, scattered in other media, were my attempt to portray the wonderful everyday life Stella and I had living in that beach house in that small south Mississippi town on the shore of the Mississippi Sound.

The stories containing the dogs provided the essence of those times. So I have gathered these scattered stories together into this anthology to give a sense of the joy we have had with these dogs, as well as to reflect on those times.

As I write this, Stella and I are at a hiatus in our lives. For us to have another Weimaraner is impractical at this time; the beach house is gone, totally washed away by Hurricane Katrina's storm surge. In the years that lie ahead, we plan to settle again in spacious surroundings that will allow us to have another of those wonderful dogs that for so many years enriched our lives.

Note that, although the several dogs were all Weimaraners, each was endowed with very special, very distinct characteristics. Their differences are part of the charm of these stories, and I have set them down in this book in the sequence that they entered and departed our lives.

In the pages ahead, please enjoy meeting and getting to know Gretal, Heron, Lillie, and Jennie, as well as spending a few short moments with Heidi, Annabelle, and Nancy. I hope their antics as we and they lived together in the beach house will please you as much they pleased Stella and me.

Paul Estronza La Violette
In a FEMA trailer on the beach,
Waveland, Mississippi,
March 2007

SAILING WITH GRETAL

All of what I am about to say here happened long before they replenished the sand on the beach in front of our house. Although the beach then was narrower, it was a wonderful time since we were able to leave our boats secured to posts imbedded in the sand.

The result was that it was a magnificent era for sailing and the beach had about a festive look, what with a number of Hobbie Cats (catamarans) and Sunfish (small lateen-rigged sailboats) tied to the posts waiting to be taken for runs in the afternoon's onshore winds. While I hoped to one day own a Hobbie, I was content with sailing a rather old and badly bruised Sunfish and, if I do say so myself, I was very good with it.

In later years, what with the expensive replenishment of new sand and the county supervisors' desire to keep the refurbished beach looking clean with expensive mechanical sweepers, these beach moorings were no longer permitted. This was a loss in many ways. Most of the boat owners found that it is just too much trouble to take their boats down to the water each day and rig them for a few hours sailing. As a result, they used their boats less, fewer sailboats sailed the waters, and the era of a skyline dotted with sails came to a close.

But I'm speaking of before this. In those sun-drenched, wondrous days, I would go down to the water after work, carrying just the Sunfish sail and mast, and quickly rigging these on the hull resting expectantly on the sand, take off for a short sail.

When I went, I would take Gretal, our old Weimaraner, to sail with me.

The best of these old days were when Gretal and I went "storming." This happened whenever a small afternoon storm sprang up and, calling Gretal (I needed her 90 pounds as ballast), I'd swiftly rig the Sunfish and, with her jumping skillfully in, the two of us would race out to the deeper water and run the winds of the afternoon storm.

I had "cheater gear" scattered about the boat to help me do what we did: grippers to hold the sail's playout, an extra long centerboard, and an extended tiller. This last was so I could hike out further with one foot on the side of the boat and the other wrapped in a bungee cord tied to the cockpit.

Gretal and I were experienced at all this, and once the sails were up, it was no time before we were moving in an exhilarating run through the rough sea, the two of us against all the forces the wind and water would throw at us.

Despite all our skills, we usually managed to press things a little too far and we would get into trouble in the middle of a screaming reach. The boat would overturn, throwing Gretal and me into the water amid a confusion of sail and hard hull. When I came up, sputtering, gasping for air, I would find Gretal paddling around in the rough sea, patiently waiting for me to right the boat.

This wasn't always easy.

The wind was strong and since the water was fairly shallow, it would push the upright hull through the water as if it were a sail, and in doing so would drive the mast into the shallow bottom. When this happened, I would have to dive down and, standing in the dark and muck at the bottom, pull and tug to get the mast loose and then quickly come up, gulp air, and then work to right the boat before the wind caused it to happen again.

Then I would climb, more accurately, slither in, pull Gretal back aboard. She would lick my face, and we would take off for more of the same.

Sometimes when Gretal and I went storming, the storm would win, and we came back losers. We returned with a torn sail, once a bent mast (this was when we crashed into Carrere's pier and that time, I still feel, was definitely Gretal's fault), and another time a broken tiller. One time when I had a hard time righting the boat, Gretal decided she was tired and swam in the middle of the jumbled sail and rested. I had to yell at her to get her out so I could right the boat.

I have on one occasion lost the rudder. I'm not sure how that happened, except it became unshipped and was gone when we got back in the boat. I lowered the sail, tied the painter around my arm, and swam back to shore, towing the Sunfish behind me with Gretal barking needless, unbelievably absurd commands from the cockpit.

This was fun, and we both loved it. She was great company and would always be eager to go out with me. Even when there were no hard winds, the two of us would go out and chase birds off the scattered pilings. She stood on the open bow or the area aft of the cockpit and bark insults at the birds. Her rough paws were ideal to keep her footing and locking her knees, she would stand secure as I maneuvered to better address the birds. Once, however, I turned too abruptly and had the incredible sight of her flying stiff-legged off the boat, as if in some Wile E. Coyote cartoon, a look of wide-eyed surprise on her face just before she hit the water.

There were many birds that we tried to scare this way, cormorants, pelicans, sometimes when we were desperate, even gulls. But of all the birds we liked to chase this way, the one that gave us the most pleasure was the Great Blue Heron. This Great Blue is a bird that stands an impressive four feet in height and has a wingspan of seven feet. This is a formidable bird indeed, a bird that attracts your attention when you see him, a bird with an attitude problem, reflected in its life style and general demeanor.

First of all, in these natural settings we did not find these birds to be the introspective heron pictured in the famous Audubon print, or the tall, very stately pairs in Le May's prints. The birds we saw were hunched-down, solitary beings who, above all, wanted to be alone. This was quite a change from say, the pelicans who were almost always in sometimes small, sometimes large, but always very civilized, social groups. Or the noisy, always fighting, gregarious large bands of sea gulls. The Great Blue seemed to prefer only one company, its own.

And alone they stayed, beautiful to see especially in silhouette, or perhaps slowly pacing, a leg lifted, then placed forward, a step, then another, hesitatingly, but sedately and always alone. If you were to drive the beach road the six miles west from our house to Bayou Caddy, you would pass many herons of different types scattered among the population of birds along the way. But the Great Blues would be spaced at 300-yard intervals from each other.

You see them either sitting on a pier or a post in the water, or in the shallows close to shore, never walking on the sand or dry beach. They appear on their perches to be hunched over, their necks sticking up eight inches below their bunched wings (Stella says they look like old men in bad-fitting overcoats). And alone.

This Garbo-like attitude seemed to beg for intrusion. Gretal and I in the Sunfish would delight in obliging by swinging the boat close to a piling sporting a Great Blue and, with Gretal barking and my yelling, force it into flight. Unlike the pelican or other pole sitters, the Great Blue would flap its enormous wings awkwardly and take off in a slow ponderous flight, circle for a moment, and then settle on another pole a short distance away.

I swung the Sunfish about and had another go at him on his new perch, and he would flap a few flaps, circle, and return to his original pole. But this pole was now upwind of us and a nuisance to go back to. Disgusted, we went off looking for easier, more cooperative birds, leaving the Great Blue sitting there as if nothing had happened. I guess, in a way, nothing had.

But as I said, all of this was great fun. Perhaps it was childish, perhaps immature, but since we both dearly loved it, that was all that mattered.

There was a time when I took off with a friend in the Sunfish without Gretal. When I returned sometime later, I found Stella very upset, standing on the beach.

"What's wrong?" I asked.

"It's Gretal," she said. "She swam after you. Didn't you see her?"

"No. Where is she now?"

"I don't know!" she cried. "She went out after you. I couldn't stop her! She wouldn't listen to me!"

She pointed exasperatedly toward the water. "You kept going back and forth, and she kept trying to catch up. Then I lost sight of her." Stella had the binoculars with her, and I took them and looked out over the water. I didn't see Gretal.

I went back out in the Sunfish to look. Since the current that day was to the east, I went all the way to the Bay looking for her. I didn't see her there and came back sailing parallel to our beach, calling her name and looking. But sitting in the low freeboard of a boat doesn't allow you to see very far, and I finally turned and headed in to where Stella was still standing.

Gretal was not with her.

We stood there for about an hour pacing about, asking people walking on the beach or in cars if they had seen her. We really didn't know what else to do.

In desperation, more of wanting to do something rather than with any hope of success, I went back out in the boat and looked around again with no luck. Just as I returned and was pulling the boat up on the sand, I heard Stella shouting. I ran to where she stood pointing.

"There's Gretal!"

"Where?"

"There! See? Down the beach!"

I looked. Finally, I made out a speck coming down the sandy beach from Bay St. Louis. I quickly got the glasses and looked. It was Gretal!

We waited, and she came up to us, and we hugged her, and she licked us, and we hugged her some more. She was wet, tired, and full of sand and so were we. Stella took her to the house for a hose bath, and I stayed to take in the sail.

I was tired and took my time securing the boat to the post and folding up the sail. I sat on the Sunfish for a few minutes looking out at the water. It had been a long day.

Finally, picking everything up, I carried them up toward the house. When I got there, Gretal, washed clean, was lying on the warm planks of the porch, letting the sun dry her coat. I sat down beside her and watched her as she dozed. It had indeed been a long day.

Gretal continued to go out with me for many years after that, and we continued to have a lot of fun together. But as she got older, I had to leave her on the beach more and more. It wasn't as much fun without her and after awhile I didn't go out as much either. When she passed away several years ago, I stopped going out altogether.

WE SETTLE INTO COASTAL LIVING

Gretal was our first Weimaraner. She was a noble-looking German pointer with a silver gray coat and hazel eyes. When we bought her, we were living in a two-room rental unit in Diamondhead, a few miles outside Bay St. Louis and Waveland. We thought then that we would be in our new home in Waveland within a couple of weeks. Our builder, however, was at the start of a long series of delays, and it was six months before we were finally able to move in.

While at Diamondhead, this at-first small puppy grew bigger and bigger. She seemed content in the small apartment waiting for us during the day. Then, when we got home, she would release her pent-up energy in wide-ranging, racing runs on the broad, park-like grounds between our condo and the Diamondhead Country Club.

There were some geese there near a large pond and they walked about the grounds as if at a large French manor. Most notable of these was a large fierce gander that would intimidate both Gretal and us when we went near the pond he ruled. We avoided the bird as much as possible, but it seemed that wherever we wanted to be, he was there.

Shortly before we were to leave, I watched Gretal, now a large 45-pound ball of energy, stray too near the pond in one of her long circling runs. Whoosh! Out of the reeds came the gander. With a great flurry of wings and whipping beak, the bird threw Gretal to the ground. Gretal rolled over in surprise under the vicious attack, but this time she kept rolling and then, reaching up, grabbed the bird by the neck. In seconds, with a big splash, the two of them rolled out of sight into the deep end of the pond.

I ran to the pond edge. Gretal was holding the gander under water, obviously intending to drown him. I yelled at Gretal; she just shook the large bird harder. I jumped in the pond and, with a great deal of confused splashing, separated the two. The gander pulled himself ashore and groggily waddled away as I held onto Gretal, who snarled and tried to break free.

We stayed at Diamondhead for a couple more weeks before moving into our finally completed house. I often saw the gander at a distance watching us. He strutted about, softly clucking a long monologue with himself, his flock carefully behind him, but he never came close enough to allow Gretal to finish their conversation.

***

After moving into our new house, Stella and I fell into the routines of making the house into a pleasant beach home. I worked outside establishing a lawn and flowerbeds, and Stella worked inside merging our two separate households of furniture into a livable collage.

On Saturday mornings, she would send me to get several loaves of fresh French bread. I would take Gretal and we'd drive along the beach road to the bakery on Coleman Avenue. At the bakery, the woman would give me the bread and a dozen glazed donuts. Then she would walk with me out to the car where Gretal would sit "pretty" and the woman would give her a sugar donut, all the time "oohing" and "aahing" and telling her what a good dog she was. Gretal already knew this, but she would wag her short tail appropriately and, after licking the sugar off her jowls, she would try to lick the woman's hand.

When we got back to the house, Stella and I would have breakfast with four or at most five of the donuts, and then I would go outside and start in on whatever Saturday yard work had to be done. Later in the morning, I would get a craving for another donut and go back in the house. Invariably I found Stella had had the same urge earlier, and the donuts were all gone.

This went on for a long time – almost a year, I believe – me buying donuts on Saturday, eating some at breakfast, and Stella gulping the remaining donuts while I was out working in the garden. One morning, as I started outside, I thought, *Why not take some of the donuts now and hide them so that I can have them later?* I turned and headed back to the dining room.

The donut plate was bare! This was impossible! I heard a noise and saw Gretal's haunches disappearing into the family room. I raced after her. I must explain that our house was a square built with a glass-covered atrium. Gretal knew this and was now trying in her effort to escape to make it to the hallway where she could have a greater fetch in the lap around the atrium. As she sped up and tried to make it into the hallway, I dove and grabbed her by her back legs. She kicked. I held on and she fell down heavily on her side. Her head swiveled around to look wide-eyed at me, her mouth bulging with donuts.

Stella came running out of the master bedroom. "What's going on?" I stood up, panting and pointed to Gretal. "That dog…" But now, Gretal, knowing she was in trouble, had broken loose and was gone.

I raced after her, yelling at Stella to close the family room door. Confused, she didn't and I had to chase Gretal twice around the atrium before I got her down again. I found that she had used her free period well and had swallowed all the donuts; there was nothing in her mouth.

She now began to pretend that she had forgotten why I was chasing her and, leaning forward, tried to lick my face.

**

Unfortunately, the baker retired and Stella began sending me to Pass Christian for bread, which was a few more miles away but had the added advantage of having the Pass Christian shrimp fleet in the harbor. So on my trip, I could buy some shrimp in addition to the bread and make a great banquet out of our late breakfast, early lunch.

Gretal and I would buy the bread, still warm, at the Pass bakery (no donuts, too bad for Gretal) and then go to a retailer/wholesaler on the Municipal Pier to get the shrimp.

That is a place, always busy, boats just coming in docking their night catch of shrimp. Sometimes, I find the shrimp a little high, but the retailer, a friendly easy-going person tries to soften the price with "they're fresh, just brought in this morning." When I look at them, I see that they are about a twenty count (twenty shrimp to the pound), which is very good, and I get a pound. When I get back to the house, I find Stella has cooked some wild rice and made a tomato salad with tomatoes from her garden and some excellent balsamic vinegar.

She compliments me on the size of the shrimp and while I set the table in the dining room she proceeds to finish fixing the meal. First she butterflies and seasons the shrimp and then pan fries them in virgin olive oil, placing the results on a large platter with the rice.

We sit down to eat, looking out the windows at the place where much of the food on the table was caught. The show of the food on the platter in the center of the table is both delightful to see and mouth-watering. I uncap a dark, heady beer that goes good with well-seasoned shrimp, put my bare feet on Gretal's back (she's under the table; she didn't get her donuts, but maybe something will fall), and enjoy a good meal.

PICTURE, PICTURE ON THE WALL

A year, then two years, went by and we settled in to enjoy the relaxed benefits of both beach living and the ambience of a small town. With only 4,000 people in Waveland, we quickly got to know many of the people in town and they got to know us "as the people on the beach with the Weimaraner."

One evening, a friend called and said he had found Gretal walking on the beach. Since Gretal was lying at my feet during this conversation, I told him he was mistaken. But he persisted and finally, I got in the car and drove to his place. Sure enough, there was a young Weimaraner, smaller than Gretal, but a nice-looking dog.

My friend insisted I take the dog as he had only taken her in because of me. I took the dog home and, not knowing how Gretal would react, put her in the garage. When Stella got home, she heard the dog's loud barking and, looking through the small window in the garage door, asked me why I had put Gretal out there. Gretal, who was standing beside her all this time, heard her name and gave a loud "Woof," and Stella jumped.

I laughed and, letting the dog out of the garage, told Stella what had happened. We watched to see how the two dogs got along. Gretal sniffed at her and when the new dog assumed a proper submissive stance and, having settled who was who, the two proceeded to enjoy each other's company.

Later, Stella, looking at the dogs sleeping by one another on the living room rug, said, "So now we have two dogs."

"Well, they look like they get along just fine," I said. "Two dogs are company, it's three dogs that make a quarrel. Don't worry, I know better. We'll never have three dogs."

The new dog was a lovely thing, and we called her Heidi. She was good company for Gretal while we were at work and the addition of another dog soon became part of the effortless seam in the way we were living in our house on the beach.

However, let me digress for a moment. When Stella and I got married twenty-five years ago, it was quite an event, and the environment encapsulating our marriage then was completely different from the warm beach environment we were now living. We were married in a small farming/mining town in western Pennsylvania on a rather cold day in December.

It was a Polish wedding. Polish weddings, like Polish funerals, are grand festive occasions. They serve as an excuse for people to gather and see other members of their family they haven't seen in awhile and they make good use of the gathering.

Our wedding lasted for two days, and I was told that, if it had been summer, it would have lasted three days. It was a grand time. Hectic, noisy, boisterous, with much drinking and dancing. Stella and I enjoyed it, and I think the people who attended enjoyed it as well.

At least the photographs of the event indicate they did.

There were a lot of photographs taken of the wedding by a professional photographer and they all turned out wonderful. Some of the photographs were funny, some just collections of people looking at the camera, looking solemn, some just people eating or dancing. But they all indicate we and our friends and relatives were having a good time.

But the best picture to us was the one of Stella and me standing at the altar waiting to declare our vows.

I'm standing there, a youthful forty-five, with just a touch of gray in my stylishly long sideburns. Beside me in filmy white, stands my much younger, beautiful bride. Behind us, there is a large picture of the Annunciation with the angel pointing up to a dove radiant in the heavens.

Its symbolism that this was a marriage made in heaven had obviously been used by the photographer many, many times, but it still to us was, and is, a beautiful picture.

We left almost immediately after the wedding to live our new lives in Mississippi. Here, we built our home on the shores of the Mississippi Sound in the small town called Waveland.

In our new house, we found the perfect place for the picture: on the wall of the dining room. From where it hung, it faced a sliding glass door that looked out across the small two-lane county road to the beach and the bright sunny waters of the Sound.

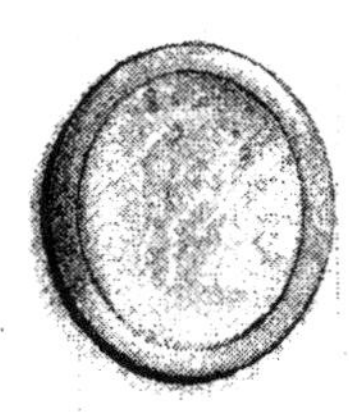

We put the photograph in an oval brass frame, twenty inches tall with a domed glass. It looked very elegant, sparkling in the sunlight on the wall of the room, and Stella and I were rather proud of it.

But Gretal wasn't.

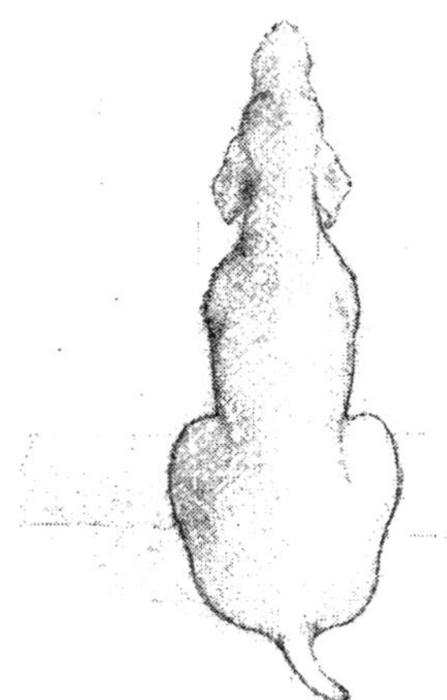

One morning as we sat at breakfast we were startled to hear a long, low growl come from under the table. I looked at Stella and she looked at me. We looked down and there was Gretal staring at something and every so often letting go a prolonged growl. We then looked to where she was staring and saw nothing at first, but then both of us realized she was growling at the picture.

"Maybe she doesn't approve," Stella said in amazement, staring first at the picture and then at the dog.

This was the start of many such confrontations between Gretal and the picture.

It did not happen all the time, seemingly only when the mood hit her, mostly in the evening and on bright clear days. She would be walking by the wall or lying under the table, and suddenly begin to emit these low growls.

It was about a year later that we got Heidi.

Heidi was a different dog than the massive, nearly 100-pound, gruff Gretal. She was a petite 60-pounder with a silver fawn coat, very pretty and quite demure, a lady, dainty with perfect manners and a kind, gentle disposition. The best analogy I could think to compare her to was someone's maiden Aunt Jane. When she ate, I expected to see a lace napkin folded by her dinner dish.

So it was to my complete surprise when one day I found her in the dining room snarling viciously at the picture.

She was a changed dog. Any vestige of Aunt Jane was gone!

She sat on her haunches looking up at the picture, her teeth bared, her hair raised on her mane, every so often letting go with a hard snarling growl. Behind her under the table Gretal lay, letting out a low growl or soft bark chiming in her agreement and moral support.

These confrontations between the two dogs and the picture continued for some time. It became so routine that after awhile we started to ignore it. Then one evening, as I was reading in the living room, I heard a loud thud of something hitting the dining room floor and saw Heidi dash by me heading for the dark safety of the front bedroom.

When I got up and went the short distance to the dining room, I found our wedding picture had been knocked from the wall and was lying on the rug. Gretal was backed up under the table staring in disbelief at what Heidi had done.

I knelt down on the floor and picked up the picture. By some miracle the dome glass had not broken.

I'm not sure exactly why I did what I did next, but still kneeling, I raised the picture up toward where it had been hanging on the wall. Suddenly, a small bright light, like a tiny firefly, darted out of one side of the lower part of the picture and raced across to the other side.

I was so startled I almost dropped the picture. Then it happened again! I broke out laughing.

I got up, rehung the picture on the wall, and then sat down on the floor below the picture and looked up. More fireflies darted across the bottom of the picture. Gretal came out from under the table and, sitting down beside me, looked up at the picture and growled.

"Stella!" I called. "Come here, I want you to see this!"

She came and, at first stood surprised at what Gretal and I were doing, then, finally listening to my plea, joined Gretal and me on the floor and looked up to where I was pointing at the picture. In seconds, a tiny firefly of light raced across the picture to the other side. Moments later, another raced back.

Stella gasped and then broke out laughing and so did I; and Gretal, not thinking it at all funny, growled.

I got up and went and got a hammer and a picture hanger and as a group we all went in procession to the entrance hall carrying the picture. There I found a suitable location and, with Stella's "a little bit over, now down, just a touch," hung it on the wall.

It seemed that at night, the tiny reflection of a car's headlights passing the house on the county road would appear to the dogs as if tiny fireflies were racing back and forth across the lower portion of the domed glass. In the same manner, on a clear bright day, the dark reflections of passing cars appeared as if beetles were scurrying back and forth.

At our normal standing or even sitting heights, the curve of the dome prevented us from seeing the reflection of the cars or their headlights.

The picture hung in its new location in the hall ever since. It appeared to be in an appropriate place for guests to see and to admire when they entered our house.

Gretal and Heidi seemed to approve as well and, although we have had several Weimaraners since, none has growled and certainly none has ever leapt up in a snarling rage and knocked our wedding picture from the wall.

AND THEN WE HAVE HERON

Heidi was good company for Gretal while we were at work. Unfortunately, a year or so after we got her, Heidi died in an unfortunate accident. We missed her, and finally decided to breed Gretal and keep one of the litter as a replacement for Heidi.

This turned out to be Heron.

Heron had a beautiful, silver-fawn-colored coat, lovely long, almost exquisite, eyelashes, and a velvet, genteel manner. She was without question a complete lady and an excellent replacement for the spinster Aunt Jane that had been Heidi.

Despite her beauty and delicate manners, there was something strange about Heron. As a marine scientist, I can best describe her as being calibrated just a little bit left of center. Stella, more diplomatic, suggested that Heron didn't always seem to be completely with us.

When this first litter of puppies (with Heron among them) came, we went over to a neighbor and borrowed the welcome box they used when their German shepherd had puppies. We kept the puppies in there initially and let Gretal tend them. As they grew larger, however, we began to take them out on the front porch to exercise and feed them.

This was good training and easy to do. Before I fed them, I put them at one end of our 12-foot wide and 55-foot long porch and ran to the other end with their food. They would chase after me, thus getting the exercise that I wanted them to have before they ate.

Invariably in their run down the long, wide porch, Heron would begin to drift to one side and before making it three quarters of the way, sometimes even before then, she would fall off. When we picked her up, she always looked at us in her dainty fashion, completely confused as to what had happened.

Keep that portrait of Heron in mind while I tell you about Heron and the crab pots.

One advantage of living on the beach is that you can put out one or two crab pots and catch your own crabs. The people here on the Gulf Coast like to boil their crabs, seasoning them with a New Orleans-made spice called "Zatarain's." Many people have special propane gas burners outside in the back yard for cooking crabs. They place large pots on these low-set gas units and, bringing the water to a boil with the Zatarain's in it, dump the crabs in as needed for a crab boil.

Stella prefers to steam our crabs the way they do around the Chesapeake Bay area, that is with lots of salt, a little bit of water, or beer, in the bottom of the pot, and to use "Old Bay," a Baltimore seasoning, as zest. One of the advantages of this method over that of our coastal neighbors is that very little water is needed and the pot can be quickly heated to produce the required steam on a normal house range.

This method comes in especially handy when we catch just a few crabs in our trap during the week. These two or three crabs can be cooked and introduced as part of the regular meal. Stella cracks and cleans them in the deep sink in the kitchen, throwing the shells into the garbage disposal. Then she serves them at the table as a sort of antipasto and there is very little mess.

In this way, we were able to include the crabs in everyday meals with very little to do. I've included Stella's recipe for steaming crabs on the opposite page. It's from her cookbook, *Blueberry Peaches, Red Robin Pie.*

STEAMED CRABS (EASTERN SHORE STYLE)

1 large steaming or canning pot
1 qt. water
2 dozen live blue crabs
1 box rock salt
1 small box Old Bay Seasoning
1 qt. beer

Place insert in pot and add water. Place pot on heat and bring water to boil. Place one layer of crabs atop insert. Put lid on pot (the heat will usually calm the crabs down). Remove lid and sprinkle crabs liberally with salt and some Old Bay Seasoning. Put in another layer of crabs, cover with lid; uncover and sprinkle salt and Old Bay. Continue layering in this fashion until all the crabs and seasoning are in pot. Add beer, cover and cook for 15 to 20 minutes. Remove crabs and serve them on a large tray on an outside table covered with newspaper or butcher paper.

Serve with separate bowls of pure vinegar and drawn butter and lemon juice. You can also make a dry mixture of salt and Old Bay for dipping.

Steaming rather than boiling the crabs helps them retain more of their fat. The salt and the seasoning adhere to the crabs and this adds to their general flavor as you crack and pick each crab.

Some people like vinegar with their crabs, others like butter and lemon juice. The vinegar enhances the already sweet taste of the crabmeat, while the butter and lemon juice just makes everything taste better.

We put our crab pots at the end of the pier belonging to our neighbor Herb. Here is where Gretal and Heron come in. In the late afternoon, the two dogs would accompany me on Herb's pier when I went out to get the crabs caught that day and bait the pots for the next day's catch. I would pull the pots up and stick in the bait – fish heads or chicken necks – and sort the catch for keepers and discards.

Gretal would jump off the pier to catch the discards I threw back in the water. Sometimes she caught one and bit down hard, cracking open its shell before it could nip her with its claws. Then she took the whole crab back to the beach and ate it, shell and all. To me it was mazing; their waving claws never seemed to faze her. I've even seen her go after large ones that I've dropped accidentally on the sand and do the same thing. She never seemed to get nipped or develop a tummy ache from the shells.

Nothing lasts forever and, unfortunately, Herb's pier was no exception. We do have vicious storms on the coast and as the pier deteriorated under the storms' pounding and the planks became lost due to storms, the gaps between the planks you could walk on became bigger and bigger.

Gretal with her weight was no greyhound, and when the missing planks left spaces more than four or five feet across, she quit the pier and waded and swam alongside as Heron and I worked our way on top. Heron would continue to leap the spaces while I would jump the smaller spaces or walk on the lengthways beams supporting the planks; the buckets I was carrying providing balance.

As more storms came and went, more planks were lost and the gaps between the planking grew wider and wider. Heron kept on coming out with me, leaping across these increasing distances. I counted the boards missing one time and figured one of the gaps was about ten feet and there were about two others only slightly smaller.

But these distances seemed as nothing to Heron. She would start at the shore side of the pier with me and race ahead, leaping the open spaces with a beautiful rhythm until she reached the square platform at the end where she would wait for me, a beautiful dog proud of her grace and skill.

But the storms continued and more planks were dislodged and the storms eventually won.

When Stella and I went to the pier after one storm, we could see there were an unusual number of planks missing. I tried to stop Heron, but she had already left our side and was racing to the pier. Her momentum carried her halfway down the length of the pier, each of her leaps covering unbelievable distances. She was beautiful to watch, touching down on two, sometimes only one plank and then leaping the next space on and on with a ballet grace.

Then there was a gap too wide for even her to vault and she fell down with a hard splash into the water. We ran to help her. She seemed confused, and Stella gave her a lot of "there, there's" and took her back to the house. I stayed and went to where Gretal was barking at the end of the pier informing us that we were missing all the crabs.

LILLIE TWO TOES

Gretal was really much too big for a Weimaraner show dog, but we decided to continue to breed her anyway since we had access to a good stud. Soon she had three more litters of very good puppies, and we became adept at breeding and selling Weimaraners.

We really only broke even as to costs (ignoring sweat equity), but we enjoyed breeding the puppies and so it seemed did Gretal. As Heron came of age, we decided we would do both Gretal and Heron with the same stud since Heron came in season a week or ten days later than Gretal.

And as lagniappe to all this, we got to play with the puppies as they grew up. These were intelligent dogs, and the things they would do provided us with surprises and much joy. Copying Gretal's earlier trick, they often took advantage of the circuit they could make around the atrium using the rooms and hallway. One puppy especially used the circuit to great effect. About four months old and named Annabelle Lee, she would prowl through the house looking for something to start her special game. She often found it on a low table in the front room that we used to assemble jigsaw puzzles.

Stella and I would be in the kitchen talking, when Annabelle's tearing through the room would inform us that the game had started. If we ignored her, she would make a lap around the atrium and come tearing through the room again.

It was an act that we couldn't ignore.

"She's got something, Paul," Stella would cry. "Stop her!"

And off I would go chasing her around and around the atrium until one of us was wise enough to close one of the doors and I would grab her and with many a growl and twist would have her spit out the piece of the jigsaw puzzle she had prized in her mouth.

Several days later she would come running through the kitchen again, and we knew she had something we had better rescue, perhaps another puzzle piece, perhaps something else. And with a lot of yelling and noise, the game would be afoot. It wasn't till after she was gone, that we realized how much we enjoyed our little game with Annabelle Lee, and that we wouldn't be able to play it with her again.

After a few successful litters, we became worried about Gretal. Things had not gone as well as we would have liked with the last litter and sure enough, we quickly started to have problems with the new litter. The puppies started dying very rapidly and after two very wretched days, only two were left. Too late we realized that Gretal's milk lacked sufficient nutrients to feed the puppies. They had literally starved to death.

I tried to save the two remaining puppies by slipping a tube in their stomachs and force feeding them. This required a certain practiced skill and had to be done every three or four hours. I placed the puppies in a shoebox that I took to bed with me to feed during the night, and to work with me to feed during the day. It was both demanding and exhausting work.

Despite my best efforts, only one of the two puppies lived. I realized that this puppy was the strongest of the litter and did my best to keep her alive. When Heron finally had her puppies about 10 days after Gretal had hers, I placed Gretal's surviving puppy in with Heron's litter.

It was a pitiful sight. Although almost two weeks old, the puppy was half the size of Heron's newborn pups. For a brief while, I had to make sure she had a teat to suck. But she quickly gained in strength, if not in size, and was soon pushing the other pups aside and getting a teat by herself.

Later, when we had the puppies up for sale, a woman came to the house and pointing to Gretal's pup, said she wanted that one. "Okay," I said and marked the dog's two front paws with nail polish.

"Your dog," I told her, "is 'Two Toes'."

We always marked the litter that way and named the dogs according to their red nail polish marking. One would be called "Back Spot," "Right Ear," "Hind Leg," and so on. Some people actually kept the name after they took the dog home.

After two months, the dogs were ready for the owners to take home and the woman came by with her small son. The boy was a seven-year-old and made a lot of noise when he came in. He was in a hurry and wanted to take the dog and go. He ran after Two Toes and tried to grab her. Terrified, Two Toes ran and hid under the couch and wouldn't come out despite his yelling.

When I saw this, I turned to the woman and said apologetically, "I'm sorry, we've been watching Two Toes and I'm afraid she's defective. As I told you, we guarantee our dogs. I'd rather not sell this puppy to you and have to buy it back later after it became ill and you've grown attached to it. Would you mind picking one of the other dogs as a replacement?"

"No! No!" screamed the boy, jabbing at Two Toes, who had gone even farther under the couch. "I want this one!"

"Don't worry, Honey," his mother said. "You can have her." She turned to me, "We want a female. Since that is the only one you have, we'll take it."

"I'm sorry," I said, "but we had a lot of problems with that particular litter. We can't sell you this dog. As I said, you're welcome to one of the other pups, but I can not sell you this one."

"I've given you a deposit!"

She was now very angry, and her voice had risen to a high pitch.

"You have to give me the dog."

I remained adamant, "I'm sorry, but I can not sell you this dog."

At this point Stella stepped in and started writing the woman a check. "We are sorry that it had to be this way. Here is your deposit back."

Handing the woman the check, Stella led her to the front door. "If you want one of the other pups, we will gladly sell you one. Think it over and if you change your mind, let us know."

She steered the woman through the entrance garden and out the large garden doors, the boy following, anxious to go to the next stop on their agenda for the morning.

I pulled Two Toes out from under the couch and sat on the floor stroking her and calming her (and myself) down. I heard the front door shut as Stella came back into the house. She put the checkbook on the table and looked at me where I sat on the floor with Two Toes.

"What are you going to call her?" she asked finally.

"Huh?" I said.

"Well, it's evident to me," she laughed, "that you now have something which you once told me that you would never have."

"What's that?"

"Three dogs. Remember: 'two dogs are company, three dogs, a quarrel?'"

I stroked Two Toes. “I’m going to call her Lillie and all she’s going to be, as far as I’m concerned, is just more company.”

And more company she was.

She was a perfect clone of Gretal, growing almost as big and with the same even temperament. After the problems with that litter, however, we did not breed Gretal anymore.

This was the practical solution to our problem. But it didn’t sit well with Gretal. She missed having puppies. For a long time afterward she would have false pregnancies and would search and search under the furniture for dust puppies.

LISTER'S POND – PART 1

Today was one of those beautifully crystal clear, autumn days, the crisp air giving a hint of the cold that will come in a few weeks.

Displays put on by the marshes and beaches on autumn days like this show the uniqueness of living on the Mississippi Gulf Coast. It makes you realize how very nice it is to live here. We on the coast are lucky to have so many places displaying this natural beauty around us. We find them in sudden openings in the brush alongside the roads in Waveland, in the Bay, and over in the Pass.

Unfortunately, we normally go by these scenes too rapidly to properly digest their beauty. We hurry by scenes of soft, almost elusive beauty that we see sometimes only by chance encounters.

Worse, we too often pay lip service to our often-repeated pledges to protect this beauty. Too often our attitude changes when that protection involves our own land, land we want filled or bolstered for a dock or some such private use.

Last week, I found this happening to a tidal pond that faces the beach a short distance from my house. In one day, heavy equipment turned a beautiful wildlife habitat that I had admired for years into something that, when the grass lawn becomes established, will more resemble an English deer park than a Mississippi coastal pond.

I was deeply saddened by this. The pond has played a strong part in my realizing the delicate role that small tideland pools play in the ecology of my immediate beach community.

I discovered this pond years ago when we first moved into our new beach house. The pond was half hidden behind some tall live oaks, marsh growth, and brush in an area I wouldn't normally go, so I never really paid it much attention. One beautiful day, Gretal became missing, and I went looking for her. As I passed the large, two-story, brick house next to the pond, the owner came out and pointing to the dark tree, bush-hidden pond, told me there is where I would be able to find my dog.

Sure enough, Gretal was in there, and I coaxed her out of the water, wet and muddy. Holding her by the collar, I looked around in wonder. Deep in the brush as I was, I could see much more of the pond than I could from the beach road.

In front of me was a small island with a tall white egret sitting regally in a large tree, posed as if for a picture. Mullet were jumping in the pond around me, indicating the pond's tidal connection, and two turtles basked on a log projecting from the water. All around me were the muted noises of a wetland in full use.

It was a beautiful place that projected a serene intimacy to the pond and its surroundings. I sat on a log for a few minutes listening to the quiet noises of the pond while Gretal burrowed with her nose after some invisible creature in the mud beside me.

When I came back out, I found John Lister, the owner of the brick house, waiting for me with a water hose. He smiled and pointed to Gretal still encased in the pond's mud. Together, we washed her off and talked. He told me the story of his house and the pond that Gretal had taken her bath in.

He said that in the very early 1800s, the pond and original house on the property was reputed to have been used as a storage area by a cohort of Jean Lafitte, the pirate. For years, this large, sprawling, wooden house was called the "Pirate House" by the locals.

Hurricane Camille in 1969 demolished any trace of the wooden structure, throwing much of the debris from the house into the pond. Lister rebuilt a two-story house using for its construction the bricks that formed the cellar storerooms of the original house; the bricks easily furnishing sufficient bricks needed for the new house.

After clearing the pond of debris, Lister let it return to its natural state as a wildlife preserve. For want of a name, the locals referred to the pond as Lister's Pond. And in fairness to the memory of my friend, it will always be that to me.

As the years passed, I had to fetch Gretal many times from either the pond or the area immediately behind it where Lister kept several Shetland ponies that fascinated Gretal. I would go after Gretal, and she would come back with me, running in large circles that included going down to the pond's edge.

Mrs. Lister liked Gretal and when she saw her on the way to the pond or the horses, she would call her up to her kitchen and feed her Belgian chocolates. When I went looking for Gretal, Mrs. Lister would call for me to come up and she would tell me of the ghost that lived in the new house.

From her second-story window, I could see the pond in the long deep shadows of the late afternoon sun. To me the scene as I saw it then recalled the coastal marshes in which I had worked as a young man. Somehow in my naiveté during that long ago time, I thought it would always be as I saw it then.

Unfortunately, I was wrong.

Mrs. Lister died and Lister remarried. As time passed both he and his new wife died and the heir broke the property into two parts, selling the house separately from the larger parcel of land that contained the pond.

A wealthy New Orleans family bought the land with the pond and, combining it with some adjacent property, began to build an extensive weekend compound.

Early one morning in late October, large trucks carrying earth-moving equipment parked on the compound grounds. Within the hour, to the surprise of the Waveland city council and neighbors (including myself), the destruction of the habitat began.

In investigating what had occurred to allow this, I was told that the New Orleans owners had approached the Corps of Engineers with the offer to swap a parcel of wetland in Pascagoula for the wetland rights to Lister's Pond. The Corps agreed.

The land clearing and paper work done and gone, we locals were faced with a *fait accompli*. There was, I was told, nothing that could be done. The New Orleans owners had apparently crossed all the right "T's" and dotted all the right "I's".

I went over to look at the scene yesterday.

Lister's Pond, as I knew it, is gone. The small island is as it was, but more exposed, and the seclusion that much of the wildlife need to breed is gone.

There is little left of the protective shoreline brush and marsh grass that bordered the pond. Soon, the local ecological fauna that depended on this small marsh/pond will find the area is no longer viable and die out. And, since the pond will no longer function as a breeding place of essential fauna, our local fishing will be affected.

Slowly, but surely, the amount of wetlands in Waveland, in Bay St. Louis, and in Pass Christian will diminish to the point where it can no longer maintain our region's rich fauna as we know it today.

When these resources disappear, the unique wonder of what we see all around us today will go with it.

And with this disappearance another part of the life we know and love will be absent from the view our children and children's children will have in future years.

Think about it.

LISTER'S POND - PART 2

There is an inherent dynamic wonder to living in a house bordering a beach on the Mississippi Sound.

From the very first days we began living here, Stella and I have been struck by the ever-changing vistas in front of us; vistas that at times lulled us to complete relaxation by their seemingly endless serenity or startled us by their shows of violent beauty.

But always there is in all scenes an ever-present vigor, a throb of vitality, of rich life.

We have learned to listen in the fall for the distinctive call of Canada geese. Sometimes these large birds will stay for a day in one of the two nearby ponds. Their call in the evening will have us running outside to see them flying high in the red, gold colors of the sky of the dying day.

Gretal loved to roam the beach in front of our house. On several occasions I noticed that she would spend time splashing in the outflow running out of the wooden culvert emptying Lister's Pond, the pond a few hundred yards west of us. This is the same pond that the wild geese and ducks loved so much.

Gretal would bark and dance about, looking at the water flowing out of the culvert, and then suddenly dip her muzzle deep in the flowing water and take large, gulping bites. Then, dancing about with her short tail whipping in a frenzy, she would look in the outflow for more of whatever she was eating.

It took awhile before I found out what it was she was feeding on; I had to look close, very close. Finally, I found it.

It, actually they, were small fingerlings, the baby larvae of fish that having reached a certain age were emptying out of the pond to continue their growth in the open waters of the Mississippi Sound.

Gretal would hover about the shallow water of the culvert's entrance during an outgoing tide and when a large group of the fingerlings appeared in the outflow, she would slurp them up in noisy, joyful gulps.

Gretal's snacks were not even an inch long. They had hatched from roe that fish had deposited in the marsh grasses that rimmed the edges of Lister's Pond. There they had grown, protected from most predators by the tall grasses. Upon maturing, they poured by the thousands through the culvert into the open waters of the Sound, there to be part of the feed of larger fish, birds and, on occasion, Gretal.

Some of the fingerlings, some very few, would escape the fate of being food to the many and grow into mature fish. These mature fish would in turn return to Lister's Pond to deposit more roe. And so the cycle would go on as it has for hundreds on hundreds of years.

These fingerlings are a major element in the food chain that makes up the ecological stock in the immediate waters in front of our house. Think of the culvert as a source of these essential feeds. As you go farther and farther from the source, the amount of food decreases and, if the immediate regional life must continue in equal abundance, there has to be another food source. Not necessarily a large source, something about the magnitude of Lister's Pond.

And so there is. About three hundred yards to our east is another pond. There, minute young fish would pour out as they matured and add to the immediate area's general food stock or replenish the region's fish.

All along the coast there are these small, but extremely vital, pockets of wetlands, each contributing its measure to the abundance of the regional fauna.

But Lister's Pond is no longer what it was.

The marsh grasses so essential to the protection of the fish larvae are gone. All that is left is a sterile tidal pond with smoothly graded sides laid out in a sort of manicured park of grass and various plantings for the out-of-state owners to come on weekends to enjoy; a park that one might find in Illinois, New York, or, in fact, just about any place in the continental U. S.

Its former unique beauty as a rich Mississippi tidal pond has been totally destroyed.

A few years earlier, the pond to our east was similarly terra-planned and its productivity drastically curtailed. As a result, the waters in front of our house depend on other small regional wetlands for both food and fish and the area is not as rich in fauna as it was in past years.

Gretal has been gone for many years now, and I miss her antics and her dance in the waters of the culvert. But then if she were here, she would be disappointed. I think this spring there will be very little coming out of Lister's Pond for her to eat.

ONE DOG, TWO DOGS, THREE DOGS

On weekends the beach road in front of the house is filled with teenagers cruising back and forth in their pickups looking at the girls on the beach who in turn are just as anxiously looking back at them. It's a busy, noisy time.

However, things are different during the week.

Weekdays, the beach is all but deserted, and the only pickups going by our house belong to workers going to job sites at homes like ours along the beach. During the time we had Gretal, Heron, and Lillie, I would take them out in the late morning or early afternoon for a swim. I did this about two or three times during the week, to give them exercise and to help keep the fleas away.

I would usually go out early in the morning, with the three of them following me in a loose, somewhat scattered pattern. The water is not deep, perhaps knee deep, and we have to wade quite a ways out, until it becomes too deep for the dogs to wade and they start to swim. It would be about waist deep to me and I would slip into a half float, my feet barely resting on the bottom and relax.

The deep water posed no problem for Gretal – she could swim for hours without any difficulty, but Heron was not the physical monster her mother and Lillie were. She would swim around for a short while gradually tiring and then, after awhile paddle over to where I floated with a pleading look on her face.

I would stop, stand in a low crouch, and extend my arm level with the water. She would swim to it and, putting both forepaws on it and panting rapidly, rest. It was a delightful, delicate moment to me, as if a butterfly had landed on my arm.

After a few moments she would be rejuvenated and pushing herself away, paddle away to rejoin the other two in swimming about doing their mysterious errands. There she would do her little busy things, until she became tired again and, turning purposely about, come back to me once again.

When I think of her today, I remember her as being so pretty and dainty compared to the other two. On those outings, I'd watch her carefully as she swam away. Finally, satisfied that she was okay, I'd lean forward and float, with just my eyes out above water, completely relaxed, letting whatever tensions I had slip away into the water.

Often a mullet would jump a foot or two clear of the water near me and fall back with a splash. Heron and Lillie would ignore the fish and its splash, but not Gretal. Gretal would immediately head for where the fish landed.

Now I knew that if a fish comes out of water, something is chasing it and that wherever it finally lands, it surely is not going to stay there. But Gretal went to the place where the fish landed in such a positive way, I felt she must surely intuitively know something that I didn't. Some bit of inherent animal wisdom. Maybe I'm wrong, I'd think. Maybe the fish was still there. Gretal would stick her head under the water and look around several times.

After awhile I would ignore her and return to my floating. I'm not sure she ever did know anything. After all, I'd seen her do that dip her head down and look many times, and I'd never seen her come up with a fish.

GRETAL AND THE PAPERMAN

When I worked for the Navy research group, I would get up early so as to be at work at seven in the morning. For breakfast during the week, I usually had fruit, perhaps some tapioca, toast, and coffee. Gretal and Heron and now Lillie would lie at my feet in the dining room.

Suddenly, Gretal would jump up. Running to the sliding glass door that opened on the porch, she would wait impatiently for me to open it and then would go flying down through the dark early morning to where a car had just stopped on the beach road.

It was the newspaper carrier. Gretal had heard the car's engine as it came down the road. Going to the driver's side, she put her paws on the door and reaching in, came out with a newspaper. The car would take off, and Gretal would run back up on the porch bringing me the morning paper.

This went on for many years. I'm not sure how she learned the trick and this was a problem, because after she was gone, my not knowing meant that I could not teach it to Heron or Lillie.

Gretal would only go to the car to get the paper during the week. On weekends, Stella and I slept late, long after the paper was delivered. On those days as I sat down for breakfast, I would open the sliding door, and Gretal would scoot out. She would go out around the side of the house to the driveway, pick up the paper, return around to the dining room door, and bark for me to let her in.

One Sunday morning she was gone quite awhile. I was about to go look for her when she appeared at the door with an enormous paper. Puzzled about its size, I took it from her and sat down to read it. It wasn't my paper; I was not looking at the Mississippi Coast's *Sun-Herald* but the New Orleans' *Times-Picayune*. I took the paper and retraced Gretal's steps around the house. As I reached the driveway, our regular newspaper carrier came up in his car and handed me our regular size Sunday paper.

"Sorry I was late. Had a little car trouble," he said and drove off.

Somehow, Gretal not seeing a paper in our driveway, or any nearby driveway, had continued to scout the neighborhood until she found a paper on someone's driveway. To her, a morning paper was a morning paper and what she had given me was a morning paper. I looked at the *Times-Picayune* in my hand. All my neighbors took the *Sun-Herald.* I had no idea where the *Times-Picayune* came from.

It was shortly after this that Gretal did not get up on a weekday to get the paper until we heard a car honk. When I opened the door, she ran down to where the newspaper carrier was waiting. He gave her the paper, and she came trotting back to me.

"New car," he yelled in his laconic way and drove off.

Soon Gretal became accustomed to the new car's engine sound and would run out and get the paper as before. It was about a year later that Stella and I met the newspaper carrier coming out of the grocery store. We talked for a few minutes as we walked to our cars. Stella pushed the shopping cart on to our car, and I stopped and told the carrier one of my many Gretal stories. He laughed, said something appropriate, and drove away.

I rejoined Stella and helped her put the groceries in the car. Then, I sat behind the wheel and tried to think through what I had just seen.

"What's wrong?" asked Stella.

"Well," I said, "that is the first time I've seen his new car in the daylight."

"It isn't exactly new anymore," said Stella. "It's about a year old now."

"Well," I said, "that is the first time I've seen his new car in full daylight. I had a good look at the driver's side door. Stella, there are long deep scratches in that door, some down to the metal. They're made by Gretal's front claws when she gets the morning paper."

"Oh, my heavens!" said Stella, "He has never said a word."

Gretchen Faustus Liebchen 1976 – 1990

ONE DOG, TWO DOGS

On those rare occasions when it snows, we let Heron and Lillie out, and they chase the big flakes, leaping, barking, frustrated at being unable to taste them once they catch them.

Once, when it got very cold and stayed that way for a week, Lillie and Heron got an even bigger shock. I took them for a run on the beach, and they headed immediately into the shallows of a low tide where they began to slip, to slide, and finally fall on the frozen water. They stood up and fell again.

Finally, by walking very carefully, they were able to make it back to the shoreline. Lillie took it all in stride and went loping away on the hard surface of the frozen sand. Heron just stood and stared at the water for a long time.

The ice was not very thick and did not extend but about twenty yards offshore. Later, as the tide came in, I watched the ice pile up in thin sheets on the shore. The next day it turned warm and the ice was all gone. But now both dogs hesitated before going in.

It's not just the seasonal things such as ice in winter. There are a lot of changes taking place in the Waveland and the Bay. Probably the biggest force for most of these changes initially was the introduction of the casinos. Casino gambling became a part of the venue of the coast in 1992. This was allowed by a Mississippi State law enacted at that time that, with the approval of local municipalities or counties, permits gambling on navigable waters within those areas.

It does seem strange that a fundamental Baptist state like Mississippi would condone such a sinful enterprise. But then one must realize that in previous years, Mississippi was a state in which bootlegging was a major, almost wide open, business when the state was dry. So I guess it should not be that big a surprise.

At this time, Bay St. Louis has one casino, Casino Magic, and Waveland has none. As a result, the Bay has new streetlights along Highway 90, newly paved roads, a better tax setup, and added revenues. Waveland has no new tax revenues, but does have the traffic congestion, the added population and, most unfortunately, the increased crime.

The police force now has more people, and more serious things are occurring on a more routine basis than in years past. But things were different back when we just had Heron and Lillie. And this is a shame. Gone are the days when a police officer would come out to the house, sit down, and, declining and then finally accepting Stella's offer of ice tea, carefully explain to us that there was a problem. Heron and Lillie had run by some old ladies and scared them and that that was going to have to stop.

Stella interrupted and asked if he wanted some of her home-made pound cake. The officer, already a bit on the round side, no longer hesitated, and the rest of the dialogue was done over several slices of cake enjoyed by both of us.

"But, Danny, I was with the dogs!" I said, waving my slice of pound cake. "The dogs were not running alone! I was driving up and down the side road letting them run alongside the car. That's the way I exercise them. They are big dogs, they need the exercise! Heck, I've been doing this for years. Heron is beautiful when she runs, you should see her. Lillie doesn't run too fast, so I'm really not going all that fast."

"You just can't do it, Mr. Paul..."

"Heck, that's absurd! This is our street. What were those old biddies doing here anyway?"

"They were just visiting from New Orleans. But you have to realize, Mr. Paul, that these ladies were frightened out of their wits when the dogs went by. They called us up and made a big fuss. We couldn't calm them down. Now, everybody at the station is upset. You know how it is. You're just going to have to figure some other way to exercise your dogs."

And so it goes. In the course of things, even in a small town such as Waveland, things change.

TRUTH AND CIRCUMSTANCE

I've been brought up on dogs being the heroes of stories; *Lassie Come Home* (the book, not the television series), *the Biscuit-Eater, Call of the Wild* ... the list is endless. All of these were stories of noble dogs loving and saving their masters from deadly peril.

As a result I came to believe that such perils constantly hover about us; that when danger threatens, it is the ever-watchful dog that will step in and, often at the risk of its own life, save us. And if there ever exists any doubt, one just had to look into the deep lustrous eyes of one's own stalwart canine and come away with the deep conviction that here is a dog that would go to any extreme to prove its love.

I believe I made it through childhood because I always had a dog. Tippy was a name a lot of them had, but I remember one with the distinctive name of Ralph. These dogs never left my side; then and now I'm sure that when I was very young, the presence by my bed at night of some long ago Tippy kept *the-thing-that-lives-in-the-closet* from coming out and getting me.

In the thirty or so years Stella and I have been living on the coast, we have always had a dog. These were all Weimaraners, noble-looking German pointers with brownish, silver-gray coats and strange, piercing, hazel eyes. Sometimes we had just one Weimaraner, sometimes more than one, but no matter the number, there was always a noble-looking dog with brownish, silver-gray coat and piercing, hazel eyes ready and willing to protect us from the evil of *the-thing-that-lives-in-the-closet*.

Or so I thought.

Weimaraners are fairly good-sized dogs commonly weighing eighty or so pounds. Although ours spent a great deal of their time outdoors, they were basically housedogs. Once when someone asked Stella why we had so many large dogs in the house with us, she replied that it was because of all the closets we had in the house. I could tell where she was going with her reply and managed to stop her before she could elaborate any further.

Actually, at bedtime, the dogs were put in the garage where they had some plastic barrels to sleep in. It was a comfortable arrangement, and they seemed to enjoy it. The barrels were deep and on cold nights two would often double up in one barrel for warmth.

***

There are times in our lives when it seems that all the values we hold sacred are tested by a single event. This once happened to me while we had Lillie.

Lillie was a lovely dog.

She had been the sole survivor of an ill-starred litter, and I had nursed her by hand to ensure she lived. She was now big and strong and when she sat looking at me when I worked on some chore in the garage, it was obvious she knew what I was doing and would help if only I would give her the chance.

The time I am talking about involved my being on the roof covering the two fireplace chimneys for the coming warm weather – we had been having problems with nesting swifts.

The work went quickly and bustling about, Lillie at my heels, I returned the vertical ladder to that part of the rear of the house near the garage, planting its two legs in a small garden. I was up on the roof for about an hour and then finished, I began to come down.

As I grabbed the edge of the ladder to make my descent, I looked down and saw Lillie patiently waiting for me. However, just as I put my foot on the top rung, the ladder started to slip away from the roof and in seconds I was dropped the nine feet to the ground.

What made it bad was that I became partially entangled in the ladder as it followed me down so that both it and I went down together. I landed on the ground on my feet, but with the ladder still tangled in my legs. It hit the back of my knee, twisting my leg and throwing me with a vicious turn, hard against the building.

I lay on my back, dazed, trying to catch my breath.

As I lay, I started to mentally check various parts of my body for pain to see if anything was broken. This did little good; everything hurt. Moving even a little bit seemed to make every one of those things hurt even more.

Then I heard a snuffling and the huge head of Lillie hung over my face.

I was saved!

I knew that I had to be badly hurt and there was no one home. But even in my dazed state I knew I was about to be saved. Lillie was here and Lillie would be the instrument of my salvation! I waited. Lillie bent forward and licked my face.

"Go, Lillie. Get help."

She hesitated, then leaned forward and licked my face again.

"Go, Lillie! Go! Go! Get help!"

She looked down at me as if trying to decide whether she should lick me once more. Then, evidently deciding she had done enough, her head disappeared, and she was gone.

I had read of this moment of truth, of the proof of the tight bond between man-and-his-dog wonder; I had seen it portrayed in a hundred movies and TV shows. I knew what was going to happen next. I felt it so strongly, it was as if it had already occurred. Lillie would go to the neighbors and somehow tell them with a bark or a pull on their pant leg that I, his loving master, was hurt and they should come. They would understand and follow her and in a few minutes, voila! I would be rescued!

I stopped trying to move and leaned back and relaxed. Things still hurt, but I knew everything would soon be taken care of. Although my chest hurt, I found that I could breathe without any problems. It was quiet. I started to doze.

Then I heard the noise.

I lay still, confused. I listened and heard it again. It was coming from the garage. It was a strange noise. It took me a couple of seconds to realize what it was.

When I did, I became enraged and, rolling over, struggled to get upright on my feet. Everything seemed to hurt. My left ankle sent pain shooting through me. I grabbed a nearby garden rake and using it as a crutch and ignoring the pain coming from everywhere else, hobbled into the garage.

There was Lillie in her barrel, sound asleep! The noise I had heard was her snoring!

When she heard me coming, she looked up startled and, sensing trouble, retreated further back into the deep interior of the barrel. I stood in front of the barrel for several fruitless seconds, banging it with the rake and yelling, but she wouldn't come out.

Finally, I went to my Ford pickup sitting in the driveway and climbing painfully in, started the engine. I would get my own help!!

It wasn't easy.

My ankle was broken, and the truck had a manual shift, but I got to the hospital where they put a cast on the broken ankle and after taking more x-rays and, to me, seemingly excessive prodding, pronounced the rest of my hurts fell under the diagnosis of "assorted bruises." Bruises that they agreed undoubtedly hurt, but still just bruises.

Despite my doubts, I was assured that I would live.

It was harder driving home with the cast on, but I did and, ignoring Lillie in her barrel in the garage, went inside and waited for Stella to come home so I could tell her about my day.

When she finally came and I told her what happened, she said that if I hadn't been so mad, I wouldn't have been able to shift gears in the truck. It was adrenalin fueled by my anger that had allowed me to do so. So, logically when you considered what happened, Lillie's actions had been the thing that had saved me.

"Saved me? Saved me? That stupid dog…"

"Stupid? She didn't come out when you hit the barrel with the rake, did she?"

"No, of course not. But still…"

"Well, I call that being a very smart dog."

And with that she left me and went out into the garage and brought Lillie back into the house.

Lillie avoided me for a couple days, but one afternoon as I sat reading on the floor with my back against the couch, she came over and sat beside me.

She sat there for a long time, very quiet, not moving, Finally, I stopped reading, closed the book, and looked over at her. Quickly, before I could stop her, she licked my face.

There are a lot of things you can do about someone you love, but staying mad at them is not one of them.

I gave her a great big hug.

JENNIE

ONE DOG

Jennie's time with us began a long time ago, but I remember it well. A friend called and told us about a woman who had a Weimaraner she wanted to give away. The woman was a traveling nurse and had found that she was not home enough to adequately take care of her large dog. We told her to send the woman over and we would see.

When the woman came with the dog, it was obvious she was desperate. We took her and her dog out to sit in the gazebo. We wanted to keep the dog away from Lillie and Heron, who were still with us and sound asleep in the garage. If we decided to keep the dog, we wanted to introduce the three together gradually.

It was a nice day and we sat, drinking sun tea and talking, while covertly looking at the dog. The dog lay beside her mistress, alternating looking at her and the water. We liked what we saw. Indeed, she was easy to like; she was a nice-looking, obviously attentive dog, about two years old, with a tail cropped a little on the long side.

In the end, we felt sorry for the woman, but even sorrier for the dog. Stella and I looked at each other and, with her nod, told the woman that we would keep the dog on a trial basis for a week. If, at the end of the week, all went well, and we didn't call her, she would know we were keeping the dog.

The woman agreed and, with many thanks, left. We took the dog inside to met Lillie and Heron.

The next morning I woke up and turned to Stella in the bed beside me, "What do you think?"

She knew right away what I was talking about, "Call the woman." she said, "Tell her we want to give her back her dog."

The problem was that the dog was extremely active. It was as if she had two interior motors and neither of the motors had an on/off switch. To be blunt, the evening before, she had worn us out.

The trouble was, she would be just one of three dogs! Remember, Lillie and Heron were two very active dogs. Three dogs are a lot of dogs, as we were well aware. And when one of them is as active as the new dog, that's more than a lot of dogs, way more.

The dog had to be returned!

As the day progressed, we decided we would keep Jennie (her new name) one more day and see how things worked out. We agreed to be patient. That one more day was extended to another day and that day extended to another and then another and so the week came to an end and as those things do, it passed and another week began.

***

As I said this was a long time ago and Heron and Lillie are both gone and all we have left is Jennie. We are glad we kept her. She really is a wonderful dog, tall, rather handsome, with a tail as I said docked on the long side (Stella says it's long enough to get in trouble with the rest of her, in fact at times ahead of the rest of her).

When Jennie does act up, we tell her that she had better start behaving because it's getting near the end of the week. For some reason, she never seems to be worried.

With all this as background, let me tell you some stories about this dog that came and stayed. About how she became part of our family for the next twelve years; first as companions to Heron and Lillie, and when they passed away, as the sole remaining Weimaraner of the wonderful dogs we have had the pleasure to know.

BOOMALAKA! BOOMALAKA! BOOMALAKA! BOOM!

Sometimes in the deep hours of an early spring night I'm awakened by a soft muzzle touching my arm. It's Jennie. I lie for a second and listen. Then comes a soft roll of thunder to the west.

I brace myself; Jennie is soul-terrified of thunder.

Of all the dogs we've had, she is the only one that has been allowed to stay in the house at night – a relic of her accident, when I had to tend to her at night. She'd picked up chasing trucks and caught one. She's very good, usually sleeping under the desk in my office during he day and beside my bed at night.

But now she's terrified.

She sits there looking at me, a dark shape in the dark of the room. I stall for a minute. Jennie won't take my stalling. She nudges me again with her damp nose, this time a little harder.

More thunder in the distance, crawling in the night sky down the beach toward us. I know that if I don't get up, Jennie will try to get in bed with us. She's scared and weighs almost eighty pounds.

I get up and start walking groggily to the back of the house with her padding behind me. It's the weekend, and Stella and I are sleeping in the front bedroom. It's a long walk around the atrium, through the dining room, and into the kitchen. Behind me, I hear Jennie's claws clicking softly on the ceramic tile floor.

Through the kitchen window I see the lightning flashes in the west beyond Bayou Caddy. The thunder is nearer and from its sounds, coming even nearer. Every time it sounds its approach, Jennie moves closer so she can touch me as we walk.

We stop for a moment. She sits, nervously resting one of her front paws on my bare foot. I offer to put her outside on the side porch; there is an immense crash of thunder, she declines.

We walk farther back through the pantry and the dark hall of storage closets and book shelves. She stays with me, very close. When we get to the door to the garage, she balks. I open the door and order her out. She won't go. I finally push her out and close the door.

Through the small glass in the door, I see her go to the two plastic barrels near the door that when Lillie and Heron were with us, we had used as doghouses. The barrels are snug and provided a privacy that they liked. She crawls into one. Then there is a particularly loud crash of thunder almost overhead, and she comes quickly out, looking around and back toward where I stand at the door.

I snap my head back from the window and listen. Quiet, then there is a scrape and rubbing sound. She has gone back into the barrel. I think she will stay in there now till the storm has passed.

I stand and listen for a moment to make sure. Around me there has started a broad engulfing sound, a growing patter. The rain has come to join the thunder.

I start walking back through the house.

As I pass through the kitchen, the sound of the rain changes to a roar. It hammers on the atrium plate glass as if flushed from a giant hose. This will be a two-incher, I'm sure. I continue, bright bursts of lightning lighting my way through the rooms of the house, the rain continuing around me seeming to hit all walls at once.

I get back in bed and pull the warm covers about me.

Stella stirs. “Where did you go?”

“It was Jennie, she heard the thunder.”

“Oh.”

I lie there and listen. There is still thunder, but now it’s become muted as it moves away to waken people in bed in the small towns to our east. The rain has slowed and now has a persistent steady beat. I say something to Stella about the rain and the early spring plantings we had put out in front. But she’s asleep.

I listen to the rain for a little while longer and then I join her.

LORELEI AND MICHAELA AND THE OTHER DOG

When school is let out during the summer, two of my grandchildren, Lorelei and Michaela, would come and visit us for several weeks from their home in Michigan. They started coming when they were 9 and 11 years old and continued to come for many years after.

Their visits were a lot of fun for us. At first, however, we were unsure of each other — Stella and I never having had sub-teens stay in the house before, and the children being placed in a totally new environment. It was a hectic first year.

They wanted meat and potatoes. Stella wanted to serve them steamed crabs, crawfish étouffée, and fresh fish along with fresh (not canned) vegetables. The only thing they seemed to want to eat was Stella's homemade ice cream.

We weren't sure how to keep them amused. We tried to take them to see everything and took them everywhere. We went for a ride on the St Charles streetcar; we flew in a friend's plane over the offshore islands; we went on a day trip to Bellengrathe Gardens and to see the rocket testing at the Stennis Space Center. All we ended up doing was tiring them and ourselves.

But we tried, we tried hard, and, interestingly enough, we realized that the girls were trying hard as well. At the end of their first visit, they said they would like to come back the next year.

As summer followed summer it became obvious that what they best liked to do was to play on the beach and the small surf in front of our house.

One summer I bought them a small rubber raft patterned after a Zodiac, only considerably cheaper and much smaller. On its bow I wrote with an indelible pen the name "The Honorable B. Nancy" after a Weimaraner that had paid us a short visit the previous winter. They were overjoyed and worked at blowing up the boat. Michaela saw the name on the bow and pointing it out to her sister, asked me who that was. I told her about Nancy's visit.

"I was working on the porch," I said, "and suddenly I saw this dog running down the beach road towards the house. It was a Weimaraner and coming in such a determined way, I thought at first it was Jennie. Then I remembered Jennie was inside. The dog came running right up onto the porch as if this was where she was going all along. Then, without hesitation, she sat down beside me, panting, as if she had come a long way and that she was finally there.

"I looked at her. She, in turn, sat where she was and, after giving me a brief glance, she resumed her examination of the water and the passing world. She was thin and filthy. I took her around back and bathed her. Later, as I fed her and looked at her more carefully, I was surprised to see what a beautiful dog she was. And her manners were exquisite. Even Jennie, who when she met her, never disputed her presence, seemed impressed.

"However, under the dirt I found a collar with a phone number for a Bay phone. I called, and her owner said that he would come by the next day and get her. So, at least we had her company for the one night.

"When he came the next day, her owner thanked me for holding her for him and took her away. Before he left, he told me that her name was Daisy, but I knew better, it was Nancy, and there it is on the front of your new boat."

At this abrupt end to the story, they turned and stared at the boat. It was evident that the logic of what I had said had escaped them. Finally, Lorelei asked, "Pawpaw, you mean you named our boat after a dog you met on the street?"

"They named a star after a dog. Why can I not name a small boat?" I retorted.

They still did not seem to understand and stared at boat and its name some more. "But what about the 'B?' What does that stand for?" asked Michaela hesitatingly.

"Why 'B' as in 'Beautiful.' What else?" I said.

"Beautiful Nancy?" Lorelei asked. "You named our boat 'The Honorable Beautiful Nancy?'"

"Well, naming it the 'Right Honorable' seemed pushing it a little."

There was a short pause; they seemed to take that as a satisfactory explanation and, dragging the boat behind them, they went down the lawn, across the small road, to the beach to play another chapter of their continuing adventure of Captain Kirk and Spock.

Only now, despite its odd name, they had the starship "Enterprise" with them.

Stella came over and sat beside me and watched the two girls. "I know how upset you were about having to give up that dog. And I knew that that 'B' stood for 'Beautiful' Nancy. But I don't think they saw the connection with naming their boat."

"It seems logical to me. I gave them the boat. Maybe I should have told them the 'B' stood for them, too."

"How's that?" she asked.

"Well, they're beautiful too, aren't they?"

She didn't answer, and we sat on the porch and continued to watch them as they moved the "Honorable B. Nancy" out onto the open seas and high adventure.

It was also a beautiful day and remember, this was long ago. But it seems that in this way, we (and they) were able to fret away that far away summer. Looking back now, I realize we whiled a lot of summers like that.

I am surprised how fast they went by.

DUST BUNNIES

Lately, Stella has been complaining about finding small fluffy balls of fur around the house and telling me to start brushing Jennie.

Now, as I've explained before, Jennie is a Weimaraner, a sort of gray German hound with blue eyes and, as with all the dogs of her breed, has very *short* hair. So I'm quick to tell Stella that Jennie is not the one responsible for the fur, it's Holly, our black tomcat.

"It's probably both of them," she says, and that was that.

Jennie is no problem to brush. I merely take off her collar, and she becomes terrified. She's naked and knows she is naked and she's equally sure everybody can see she is naked. Until I put it back on her, she will follow me anywhere. Her tail is down, and she sticks very close to me, casting nervous glances around to see if anyone is watching.

I put her on the edge of the porch and stand in the grass in front of her. She is just at the right height and in a few moments, dodging the nervous licks she tries to give me, she's being brushed.

I use a wire brush, and it does a good job.

I will admit that Jennie does need brushing; it takes longer than I thought. I have to clean the brush a few times before I'm done. I put her collar back on, and she starts an insane puppy-like scamper around the front lawn to show her happiness.

That done, I turn around for Holly.

Up until then, Holly has expressed no interest in what has been taking place. He lies on the porch a few feet away from us, stretched out in an almost sphinx-like pose, watching the waters of the Sound, deep in an ethereal aura of contemplative meditation that only a cat can assume.

Now, what with Jennie's scampering antics on the lawn and my turning toward him, reality sinks in and Holly elects to leave. I dive and find that his tail makes a good grabbing point.

I place him on the slanting porch steps railing. He attempts to escape, moving down the railing about a foot before coming to a dead stop — I still have his tail. With him heading one way and my pulling the tail the other, he is stretched out in a perfect position for brushing, and I brush.

Now, as I start to brush Holly on the railing, I can see something that I hadn't noticed before; the short hair is getting long. I brush harder, and Holly stretches his body out further. I keep a firm grip on his tail. Now the heat of summer is here, and I realize, as I work the brush on Holly's lustrous, *long,* black fur, that both he and Jennie are shedding their winter coats. When I let him go and he joins Jennie on the grass, I can see that their glossy new summer coats look good on both of them.

Later as I vacuum around the house, I find that they have been shedding quite a bit of hair. I repeat the vacuuming later in the week, and Stella mentions not seeing any more fur balls.

Still, the ritual of the porch brushing has been taking place each weekend, accompanied by Jennie's embarrassed glances and Holly's taut body stretch.

I think, despite their antics, that they both like it.

PATTERNS IN THE SAND

When I go down for my daily walk on the beach, I think of it as an adventure of discovery. It is true they are small adventures and what I find are small discoveries, but it doesn't matter. I know each day that I will discover something different and that to me is the main enjoyment of what I do.

It starts off completely backwards from the way someone who is familiar with our household would think it should. I'm carrying Holly, who is street-wise and doesn't need carrying. Jennie, who I probably shouldn't trust since she got hit by a pickup truck several years ago, is running free.

But there is a twisted logic to all this.

I'm carrying Holly because he won't normally come with us unless I carry him. Unlike Jennie, he's scared of the cars and pickups on the road, hence his hesitation about crossing the road. When he realizes we are going to the beach, he becomes uncharacteristically still, his body flattened against the ground, letting me pick him up and carry him toward the road.

When Jennie, on the other hand, realizes we are going to go for a walk on the beach, she starts running around Holly and me in maddening tight circles acting like what we are about to do is something we haven't done in years, when actually we did it yesterday.

However she has been trained not to cross the road until I tell her, "Go" and despite her excitement, she stops just short of the road, straining in her nervous excitement, to hear the magic word.

Checking to see that there are no cars, I yell "Go!" and Jennie races across the road (of course, not looking either way) and I follow carrying Holly, who is squirming in my arms, craning about, trying desperately to look both ways. I may be the best road-crosser in the world, but it's one of his nine lives that's at stake and he'd rather double check my looking.

But all of us get safely across and we start our walk.

I put Holly down, and he immediately starts checking out minutia in the tall barrier grass that runs in two, long, parallel rows ten and twenty feet from the road. Jennie runs to the water's edge, to sniff about and maybe chase (maybe catch?) a bird or two.

I stay neutral walking the middle sand between them, strolling either toward the east or west as the mood of the day strikes me, looking at the water, the birds, or sometimes just at the sand at my feet.

I carry a small pair of Ziess 10x25 binoculars to watch the birds and things out on the water, but I don't need anything to look at the sand. I suppose, at first glance it would seem to be that all that can be said about the sand is that it's there, it's white, and the maintenance crew keeps it nicely laid out and sifted clean so that it shines brightly in the early morning sun.

It is true that there isn't the profusion of shells you would see on an ocean beach. This is, after all, the Mississippi Sound, an estuary, not the Gulf of Mexico. The only shells we normally see on our beach are the occasional *Oysteria* or that of a small brachiopod, *Rangia*. Neither is very interesting to look at the first time you see it and after you see it that first time, it gets even less interesting.

But there are patterns everywhere in the sand and at the water's edge that I find appealing and make the trips to the beach as interesting to me as they are to Jennie and Holly.

As I walk on the open area of the sand just beyond the barrier grass, I find that one of the maintenance vehicles, a large front loader, has gone by and laid two exquisitely detailed tracks in the sand. These extend in a straight line from Jeffery's pier, to my east, to the culvert emptying Lister's pond, to my west.

The two, long, parallel tracks appear to me as if someone put an elaborate crocheted border on the upper part of the beach. The exact repetition of the marking in the sand made by the treads of the heavy vehicle's wheels is amazing to see; each grain of sand seems to be in place as if an elaborate engraving. It seems impossible that something so large could leave behind so minutely precise a marking of its passage.

I am kneeling down to look at these markings more closely, when, with a swirling whoop! Jennie thunders up to me, licks my face, dances about for a second, and then races back to edge of the sand by the water and the elusive birds.

It was sort of a "Hi, I'm here. Now, I'm going to be over there, Goodbye" lick, and I appreciate the thought, but when I look at the tractor wheel's imprint in the sand, all semblance of its precise order has been blown away by Jennie's explosive passage.

I hear a slight noise and turn and there is Holly, coming from behind his grass protection to see what had happened.

His tracks on the sand are faint, but obvious. He goes to where Jennie had passed through and proceeds to roll in the exact same sand, obliterating whatever tread design was left in my immediate area. Evidently, to him, this is some kind of polite territorial thing. I'm not sure exactly what; with cats you can never really be sure, and I'm wise enough not to try.

I make my territorial statement; I flick sand at him and, still lying on his back, he waves a paw threateningly back at me. I flick more sand, and he waves his paw again.

I suppose if the sand impressions of this little tableau were somehow saved for some archeologist of the next millennium, he/she would have problems solving the story of what had taken place here on the sands of Holly's, Jennie's, and my time.

But I know it's not likely that this particular patch of sand will be saved and I get up, wipe my hands and knees, kick more sand at Holly, and go on along the beach to see what other features need discovering.

We had rain two days earlier, and the path of the water's runoff from the county road is still freshly visible as shallow furrows in the sand. I find these more interesting than the tracks of the maintenance tractor.

A close look at the furrows reveals physical forces on both a small and large scale. At first, the furrows remain fairly uniform. They show the water flowed along the rows between the barrier grass and, at the first break in the rows, turned to run across the open beach sand toward the water.

But the slope of the beach is not great and any disturbance or rise deflected the flow and, like a meandering river, the furrows reveal the water flowed in long meanders to join the water of the Sound.

Now, I'm at the water's edge where Jennie greets me.

Up toward the road I can see the tiny black head of Holly watching us from between two clumps of grass. He doesn't realize that rather than blending in, his black fur makes him stand out from his brown-gray surroundings.

Walking along, Jennie ranges away from me, sometimes in the water, sometimes on the sand. I stay on the sand looking for what stories it has to tell me. Near the edge of the water, I see that someone has been here before us this morning. There washed by small wavelets are the fresh, cleanly pressed, three-toed prints of what appears to have been a Great Blue Heron.

I put my hand atop one print and barely cover it, it is so large. There are only a few of the prints; the bird had evidently walked out of the water for a few steps then returned. Looking around I can see no Great Blue nearby, just some terns that Jennie chased a little while ago and Jennie herself looking back at me, waiting impatiently for me to go with her.

These prints as well as all of what I had seen, impacts on the seemingly sterile uniformity of the beach. A uniformity that the maintenance crews and their vehicles are vainly trying to maintain. I think they have fairly secure jobs; they are going to be doing this for some time.

Think about it. I had no trouble flicking sand at Holly. Sand is easy to push around; it's small, it's round. A shape similar to that of a tiny ball bearing.

The beach and the bottom material of the water beyond the beach is made up of billions on billions of these tiny ball bearing-like spheres and, like ball bearings, they are easy to move about. As we have seen today, in addition to the maintenance crews, the rain, wind, tide, and current are all fiercely at work doing this moving about.

This moving of the sand goes on constantly, winter and summer, spring and fall. Summer and winter storms that slip by the barrier islands accelerate the movement. While we all admire and enjoy the beach, we tend to forget the natural forces working to change it. Despite the best efforts of the maintenance tractors, the beach I see today will not be the beach I see a year from now.

However, not all changes are epochal; in fact most are minor and it is these minor changes we normally see and enjoy in my morning walks. I know that when we are asleep tonight, something will be pushing those little grains around. It may be a brief shower, a strong tide, the wind, or just a fidgety flock of restless terns. I know that tomorrow, when I take Jennie and Holly for our walk on the beach, we will find patterns in the sand for us to find and enjoy.

I call Jennie and she comes racing back to me and we head back to where Holly waits by the grass for us to return to the house. I hear a noise and look up. Very high in the sky above us, two seagulls are flying north; one a little on my left, the other a little on my right.

Their clear calls to one another as they fly high above me are unlike the raucous sound I usually hear from gulls. Their calls are clean, crisp notes as if from two finely tuned bells; one ringing on my left and seconds later the other ringing on my right.

They leave with their sounds, a clear resonance that I will take back with me to remember and place with the other patterns of the day.

TO JENNIE WITH LOVE AND WET KISSES

Yesterday I went to Waveland Elementary School to give a talk to some third grade students.

Their teacher had read several of my Sunday newspaper columns to the class and, since the children seemed to enjoy them, she had asked me to come and talk to them. When I asked her what I should talk about, she said to speak about what it is like to be a writer and the work that is involved in writing.

I know newscasters, weather people, police officers, and rehabilitated felons speak to school children all the time, but this would be completely new to me. So, when I said that I would come, I said it with some trepidation.

First of all, while I do write a Sunday column for a local newspaper and have authored several non-fiction books, I am basically a scientific writer. For example, the title of one of my papers reads, "Eddies and thermohaline intrusions of the shelf / slope front off the Northeast Spanish Coast." I'll be the first to admit this is not too exciting.

So, I felt sure that anything I would say would put the class of nine-year-old children to sleep in less time than the thirty minutes she suggested my talk should last.

I decided I needed a gimmick, something flashy. As I thought this I happened to look down. There by my feet under my desk was Jennie, sound asleep. I smiled; she would do.

I reached down and patted her rump. Her eyes opened for a brief second, and she stared up at me. Then, satisfied that I wasn't getting up to fix her lunch, she closed her eyes and disappeared back into the land where squirrels can be caught and cats do what they are told.

There are many learned treatises on the human / dog relationship. These studies point out that we often mistakenly attribute many of the human-like actions of our dogs to their association with us; we think that this association has somehow endowed our dogs with some human spark. "Did I tell you what little Rover did yesterday?" is undoubtedly the most overworked sentence in any dog owner's vocabulary.

The truth is just the opposite.

Those faithful and loving dogs that we treasure so much, far from thinking themselves human, think of each of us humans as being another dog! A nice dog, a rather large dog, and at times, until trained, a rather silly dog, but still a dog.

All this is based on years and years of scientific study and has been published in a number of very good technical journals. I'm sure that they have good investigative data for writing all this and I'm willing to give these researchers their due.

However, Jennie is now eleven years old and has been with me nine of those. Since a near decade of study is much longer and more quantitative than some vague "years and years of study," I believe I have a better handle on the human/dog relationship than those dry journal publications.

Jennie and my visit to the class is a good case in point. So from a purely detached scientific viewpoint let's see how it turned out.

***

My visit was to take place in the school library. I was there before the children arrived and had Jennie on a training collar and leash.

It's been years since she had her obedience training, but she remembers it very well. She sat, therefore, reasonably still, and watched as approximately thirty children filed into the room.

I haven't been around young children for a long time and was amazed at the orderly way they sat in a large square on the rug in the center of the room and stared expectantly first at Jennie and then at me.

The teacher spoke for a brief moment and then turned to me. I realized with a start that I was on. Trying not to wave my arms too much (I had Jennie's leash in my hand), I began my talk.

It went reasonably well. They were a good audience, and I found I could speak rather freely without having to talk down to my young audience. I spoke about writing in general and what it takes to write. After a bit, as an example, I read aloud a column that was to appear in the next week's Sunday paper.

Drawing by Ryan Gardache, Waveland Elementary student

The column was about Weimaraners, and I pointed to the patiently sitting Jennie to emphasize various points. Patient, that is, for Jennie. She would get up, turn in a circle and sit down and get up and repeat the process about every three minutes. My reading was sprinkled with a running cadence of "sit Jennie," but all in all, she was quiet.

Then after the class had asked and I had answered a number of rather surprisingly pertinent questions, I realized my talk was almost over. I decided to close it with a bang. I bent down and unsnapped Jennie's leash.

Whoosh!!

Jennie was up and leaped at the surprised square of children. Dropping her head down like she was burrowing under a rug, she plowed into them. The children, in turn, squealed and tried to bury Jennie under a mass of their bodies.

Jennie twisted and squirmed and breaking loose, ran a circle about where I sat and then from a completely different angle plunged once again into the square, producing the same result of screaming, laughing, grabbing children.

It was pandemonium and, what was nice, it was our pandemonium.

She did this several times and then it was time for us to leave. The children, once again quiet, filed orderly out of the room while Jennie restrained by the training leash sat watching them, her tongue hanging out and her head cocked appreciatively to one side. The teachers thanked me and walked me to the school entrance. There I put Jennie and my material in my car and climbing in, I drove home.

As we drove, Jennie sat still, a pose she always assumes in the car or truck. After all these years, I can't understand how a dog with Jennie's nervous temperament can possibly stay still in a truck, but she does.

Despite her pose, I could see, however, that she was still both excited and happy about the visit we had had with the children. She sat there obviously thinking about what had happened, restlessly lifting a paw and putting it back down or glancing over at me and then back out the side window.

Up paw, down paw, look right, look left.

Finally, she couldn't stand it any more and standing up, she reached over and gave me a big slobbering lick. I had to stop the car. The car behind me honked, but I didn't care.

***

There, I've presented my unbiased clinical case study. Let me see them explain that in their scientific journals.

THE NIGHT WOLFDOG FOUND HIS HOME

His name wasn't "Wolfdog" to begin with. When we first saw him, he was just another of the strays left by the summer visitors to wander the roads. He came up to the porch from the beach road and sat in front of the sliding glass door looking in. Stella and I were just inside having breakfast.

He sat patiently watching us as we ate. Stella, a pushover for strays, went out finally and gave him something to eat.

As he ate, however, even she could see that beyond that faux timid air was a more self-assured dog, a dog that was looking for a permanent home. We quickly agreed that our house was not going to be it.

We fed him and made him move on, which he did well naturedly, going on to check the other house on our side street.

Over the next few days, he became a neighborhood fixture, appearing at back doors of the various houses and giving his "I'm just a poor homeless waif, etc, etc.", act with unfortunately little luck beyond table scraps. However, when he tried his spiel at Barbara and Laura's place a little farther up the street, he hit pay dirt.

In fact, he captured Laura's heart, but not Barbara's. "No more animals," said Barbara, and that was the way things stood. At least that was the way she thought they stood; Wolfdog had a different opinion and, picking a comfortable bush on the side of their house, began his wait.

***

Late one evening a couple weeks later, Stella and I were just getting in bed when we heard a loud crash coming from the side street beside our bedroom window. Quickly lifting the blinds, we saw a car had crashed into a utility pole across the street from our house. The pole toppled half over and a woman was trying to get out on the passenger side of the car.

Stella quickly picked up the phone and called the police. I hurriedly put on some clothes and went out to see if anyone was hurt and if I could help. When I got to the car, a woman on the passenger side had already gotten out. She seemed to stagger, and I went to help her. She pushed me aside, announced she was going "back to the party," and, still staggering, but moving at a fierce determined rate, headed up the street.

I looked inside to where the driver was slumped over the seat. The smell of alcohol filled the inside of the car as well as the sound of loud snores. The driver was fast asleep! There appeared to be no blood or indication of serious injury, and I backed out, prudently deciding to wait for the emergency vehicles.

By now Stella had joined me as well as several neighbors and we all began talking at once, pointing at the downed utility pole, the car beneath it, and the woman weaving her way up the street. Then we heard yells coming from the direction of the party.

Let's forget the sleeping driver and his incapacitated car and go up the street to where the yelling was coming from. The exact events of what was happening are best told by Barbara or Laura. I will try to re-tell as best as I can, what they told me.

The party at the Dill's, across from Barbara and Laura, had been in full swing when the two went to bed. They were wakened sometime later by a loud crash from the front of their house.

Looking out the window, they saw that a car coming out of the Dill's driveway had backed up on their front lawn and hit something. With a loud squeal of tires and a revving of the engine, the car began driving away.

Barbara and Laura, both still in their bedclothes, went running out to see what had happened.

The whole scene was terrifying. They saw the car going erratically far down the street, just missing one and then another of the several parked vehicles along the road, and then smashing into something that brought it to a stop.

There was a brief moment of silence, then closer at hand, somewhere near the front of their lawn, they heard a rushing noise as if air was escaping. They turned, looking for the source of the noise. Laura saw it first.

The car had hit the gas meter and gas was hissing out of the ruptured line!

"Don't worry, lady," Laura heard a voice yell out. "I'll take care of that."

She looked across the street and saw one of the guests from the party coming over to where they stood. He was obviously drunk. In his right hand, he held a wrench. What was worse, in his left hand, he held a cigar.

She immediately started to yell at him to stay away, but he grabbed the damaged meter and told her in a loud, very slurred voice that everything was going to be all right. He would fix it.

She grabbed him to pull him away from the wrecked meter and the escaping gas. He yelled at her to get out of the way and when she wouldn't, he shoved her roughly to one side, throwing her on the ground.

Then out of the bushes, slobbering and snarling horribly as if from some vicious nightmare, came

Wolfdog!!!

Laura says that from her position on the ground, it was almost surrealistic. She remembers the snarling deep growl, the dark mass that raced across the lawn and hurled itself viciously at the startled man, noisily trying to reach his throat. She said the only thing the dark mass didn't have was a cape and background music.

The man dropped his wrench and raised his arms to protect himself. But it was no use. Wolfdog was at his moment of destiny and he knew it. He didn't need a cape, he didn't need music, he just kept coming.

In desperation and yelling at the top of his lungs in a voice that had suddenly become unslurred, the man raced back across the street to the safety of Dill's house.

Wolfdog followed, hard on his heels.

***

To us in the neighborhood watching from our lawns, the aftermath of all this looked like the end of the old Marlon Brando movie, *The Wild Ones*.

Police cars, tow trucks, utility company vehicles, ambulances were everywhere, cluttering the street, stopping, moving in an almost choreographed dance. A tow truck grabbed the end of the wrecked car and towed it away; a utility truck braced the pole into a temporary upright position.

The neighbors stood on their lawns in the dark watching; the glow of the various rotating yellow and red lights illuminating the little groups of faces on each lawn.

Finally, the last of the emergency vehicles drove away and in the silence that was left, we each went back into our respective homes. Tired from all the excitement, Stella and I went back to bed.

Up the street Barbara and Laura went in through the front door of their home and Wolfdog, their new dog, went through the front door with them.

TIDAL FLATS ON A WINTER DAY

There is a strong winter high today and the wind associated with this atmospheric high has pushed the water four or five hundred feet out from the beach in front of our house.

Highs like this in winter make beautiful days and this is one of the best of those days. This afternoon Jennie and I take the opportunity to walk (running in her case) out onto the newly exposed bottom of the Sound.

It's a strange feeling to walk on a surface that is ordinarily covered by the Sound's tea-dark waters. It's as if a plug has been pulled and the floor of the Sound has suddenly been laid bare. One expects to find strange hulks strewn about, relics of some forgotten catastrophe, old ruins, exotic forms.

In a way there are such sights, perhaps not as romantic as man-made debris, but still evidence of the powerful forces that are always at work on the waters of the Sound.

Under my feet as I walk, I see the bottom is corrugated into wave-like ripples an inch or so in height. Spread out in all directions across the exposed bottom, these ripples were formed by the motions of the water when it covered this area during the last tide.

Because of their wave-like appearance, the ripples look as if they are some mud casting of the last tide's sea surface. They are not.

Their beautiful patterns are not direct reflections of what the water's surface once looked like. Rather, their shapes are complex integrations of the many wave motions and other factors. Still, whatever their cause, their distribution about the tidal flat form delightful patterns about me.

As I walk (Jennie is still running), I see that others have been here before us.

I see the small trifurcated footprints of several snipes and, looking up, I see the birds themselves are just a few hundred yards ahead of me, walking, flitting about excitedly, looking at these same tidal flats as if it were some smorgasbord of goodies. I suppose to them it is.

A little farther on I see the undeniable imprints of a duck's webbed feet! I have not seen a duck today and looking about still find none. But here at my feet is the undeniable proof that a duck had walked in this same place within the last few hours.

I can't spend anymore time looking at these artifacts; Jennie, whizzing by me, grabs my full attention. She races by in an arc of one of several large elongated circles, whose purpose is sometimes to chase birds and sometimes to make turns that really lead nowhere.

What I see in her passage is the raw release of energy, of letting go after being pent up for too many days. Her paws rip into the mud; leaving clear prints in the rippled bottom that trace the eccentric path she follows in her loping runs.

Jennie, like the ripples, like the snipes, like the clear spotless bright sky above us, is a joy to see, to feel the vibrant life that permeates the entire broad setting in which we are walking. It is, indeed, a wonderful day, and we are here, Jennie and I, walking in that wonder.

***

Yet there are interesting facets to all this.

As I call Jennie and we go back to the house, I see that some action of the receding water has laid a wash of sand that has partially covered some of the rippled bottom.

Peppering the ripples are small holes, filter tubes of fauna that wait the next tide's flooding. These are also partially covered by the sand. If I carefully scrape away the sand, I will expose the now covered ripples and the filter holes. But I don't and the area remains covered.

In effect, all of the area covered by the wash has become part of the layer upon layer of material that makes up the subsurface strata of the bottom. Until some tidal current or storm comes along, these features will remain buried in the strata.

With the way the Sound bottom is constantly being worked and reworked by the wind and tidal currents in this area, this will probably happen in a day or so, if not sooner.

But sometimes, in rare instances, this does not happen and the material stays buried, remaining out of touch of the winds, waves, or tides of our time or even our century.

With this thought, I find myself viewing what I see about me with a different perspective. In my mind's eye I see a sandy outcrop in a narrow canyon in Wyoming that I walked many years ago on a geological field trip.

Deep in the cool shadow of the canyon, I looked for fossils to give me the geological time of the sediments that composed the tall canyon walls stretching above me toward a distant sky. The chipping of my pick dislodged a large slab of sandstone, and I stared in wonder at the fresh surface that was bared.

They were ripple marks!

There, exposed by my pick for the first time in hundreds of thousands of years, were the remains of the bottom of a shallow sea.

And imprinted on those ancient ripple marks I saw evidence that something, some prehistoric creature, had run across the exposed bottom of that shallow sea and left a long line of small footprints, footprints that had kept a clean crisp impression throughout the thousands of years since they had been put down.

That deep canyon I was walking in had once been a broad shallow sea with a bright sun and waves and currents and a tide. During one period of low water, some animal ran on it and left its footprints on the exposed sandy bottom of that sea.

Perhaps in running, it had felt the same sense of joy that I feel on this day as I walk about the tidal flats with Jennie under a crisp clear sky and a bright winter sun.

GRETAL, HEIDI, HERON, LILLIE, AND JENNIE

In the preface of this book, I spoke about my taking a nap on the living room floor with Jennie. Let me expand on this a little bit more.

I'll be the first to admit it; I take a nap during the day, usually at noon. I'm not ashamed. It's usually a crash thing that lasts between twenty and thirty minutes. I've always done this. The naps are a residue of my time in the military when I learned a powerful lesson: when you get a moment, seize it, take a nap. It is a regime that has stood me in good stead for many years.

These naps really are power naps. They refresh me. Years ago when I woke up from one, I would feel great and get up knowing I could work for another eight or ten hours smashing boulders, leaping tall buildings, etc., before needing a recharge. Now, when I get up from one, I feel like charging a herd of angry buffalos.

A very small herd of very small buffalos, but still…

As I indicated in the preface, I usually took my naps on the living room floor, and Jennie usually joined me, lying close to me and staying there till I woke up.

Her doing this is an interesting phenomenon. When we had other dogs, they did this as well. There was a time when Stella and I had three Weimaraners in the house. Mind you, these are big dogs, averaging eighty or so pounds. It seems strange to me now that we were able to have dogs of this size inside the house. But at the time, it seemed perfectly normal.

Back then, when I lay on the floor to take my nap, all three of the dogs would saunter into the room. It was a sort of ritual. Each would quietly arrange itself around me according to its position in the household hierarchy, the alpha dog near my head, the second at my waist and the third relegated to my feet. Once down none would move till I woke up.

The pattern in which they laid in reference to my position on the floor was also interesting. That is, they would lie with their hindquarters toward me and with their heads pointed out. Sometimes the head would be tucked back in my direction, but the body was always oriented away from me.

It took years for me to realize there was a reason for all this and that in doing what they did, they were paying me a very personal compliment. The pattern around me, in fact the reason they came in the room to lie around me when I took a nap, was an act peculiar to pack animals. They were forming their bodies into a sort of perimeter defense.

When I lay down and slept, I, the master, or really the pack leader, became, in effect, vulnerable, and so, befitting my status in the group, I was immediately enclosed in a defensive circle of noble canine warriors.

When viewed that way, this commonplace act by these loyal wonderful beings, that for a too short a time shared Stella's and my life, was a wondrous thing.

Since you are reading this book and therefore enjoy the companionship that dogs provide, I am happy to pass on this list of small bits of canine wisdom I got from a very close friend years ago: ——►

THIRTEEN THINGS YOU CAN LEARN FROM YOUR DOG

1. When your loved one comes home, run to greet him.
2. Take naps.
3. Eat with gusto.
4. When it's hot, drink lots of water. Splash it around when you do. Show you appreciate it.
5. Take naps.
6. Never bite, growl. If it's a friend, growl silently.
7. Give unconditional love. Do this twice each day. Increase this amount on weekends and official designated holidays.
8. Take naps.
9. Stay close to your loved one in times of stress. Get closer when things get worse. Get as close as you can when things get very bad.
10. When you want something badly, dig for it. Dig hard. Make loud noises when you dig.
11. Take naps.
12. If you are happy, show it, wag your tail. If you are really happy, wag it harder.
13. Take more naps.

Anon

A PORTRAIT OF JENNIE

I woke up last night and, finding myself wide awake, listened to the sounds of the house at night.

It's an odd thing, but there are many noises around us that we become so accustomed to that we don't really hear them. The house shifts; the air conditioning goes on and off; the clock ticks in the hall, its chimes go off on the hour with loud bongs. But mostly the sounds I heard last night were those made by Jennie, our large gray German hound.

She was snoring.

As I lay there, I realized that, like the motor of an old refrigerator, her snoring was unobtrusive. Like the clock and the air conditioning, it was there and yet not there. I could, if I wished, have fallen back to sleep without it bothering me.

Yet as I lay there listening, I realized that her snoring was loud. In a way, however, no matter how loud it was, the sound was comforting. Its presence meant to me, that Jennie was there and that when I awoke in the morning, she would still be there.

During the day, Jennie follows me around everywhere and at night she usually sleeps a short distance from the foot of our bed on her own pad. Every now and then, she wanders a bit during the night, sleeping sometimes on the small rug on Stella's side of the bed and sometimes on the rug on my side.

When I awoke last night, I found that she was on my side of the bed and I remember reaching down and touching her flank, listening to her snore.

We first started letting Jennie sleep in the bedroom after she had an accident a number of years ago. Before that she slept in the garage on a pad in an old plastic barrel with blankets added for the cold during winter. Then one week she started chasing pickup trucks passing the house on the side street. Within that week, before I could teach her different, she was hit by a truck and lay on the street, screaming in pain and terror.

When I picked her up, her front left leg was pointed awkwardly at midpoint to one side, and she was screaming in pain and shock. With the help of the pickup's driver, I managed to get her in the back of our car and, with Stella driving, rushed her to the small emergency animal clinic in Orange Grove.

The clinic was understaffed at the time, and I found myself holding the sedated Jennie while the vet drilled holes in her leg. These were for stainless steel bolts that secured the two steel rods that would keep the leg in traction and provide support while the shattered bones healed.

The trip home was slower. Stella drove, and I sat in the back with Jennie. That night, Jennie slept for the first time on the floor in the bedroom. I slept beside her to be there when she came out of the anesthetic. The vet warned me that her awakening would be rough, and it was. It was a terrible night for both of us.

Jennie's time in our house has always been a trial sort of thing. A woman gave Jennie to us because she was not home enough to adequately take care of her. We said we would keep her on a trial basis for a week. The next day we began to think we had made a mistake.

The problem was that the previous evening had shown the dog to be extremely active. She had worn us both out. And this dog would be just one of three dogs (we still had Lillie and Heron)! In the end we decided to keep Jennie (her new name) one more day and see how things worked out.

That "one more day" was extended to another day and that day to another and then another.... Years have gone by and that day-to-day dog is the same dog, now a great deal older, that lies snoring beside me in the middle of the night in this dark house.

It has been a long time.

I remember once coming home a little dispirited by the events of the day. Walking through the house, I took some sun tea from the refrigerator and went out to sit on the porch. Jennie went with me; maybe I would let her play fetch with the Frisbee. I didn't. Instead I relaxed on the lounge and thought about the day's happening. Somehow, I felt that things seemed to be getting away from me.

Jennie intruded, her spirit was too much for my tired thoughts. I looked at her. Seeing she had my attention, she dropped the Frisbee on my lap and pranced back, a broad grin spread over her face. I sat up as she leaped up and down in anticipation. I threw the Frisbee far across the lawn.

Jennie spun about, scrabbling so that the dirt flew, raced out and, leaping spectacularly in the air, caught the Frisbee about four feet from the ground. It was a beautiful catch. Of the many things I remember about Jennie, I remember the tremendous catch that she made that day and the proud bearing emanating from the her as she brought the Frisbee back to me.

There are other memories. Above all the things Jennie likes to do, she loves to go exploring with me on our beach. When she was younger, she loved the exulting feeling of freedom presented by the open spaces of yellow sand the beach provided.

When we walked on the beach, she would race ahead of me, moving at tremendous speed in broad, ranging circles, shedding some of the excess of energy that seemingly was always cooped up within her. Large circles, small circles with the sand kicked in sprays as she made her abrupt turns.

To watch Jennie then was to watch the essence of the joy of life.

Now time is with us and our walks on the beach are more sedate. Jennie still moves about; eagerly sniffing and checking the sharp smells of the shoreline, but the full roar of endless circles of shedding energy is gone.

A friend asked to take her with him as company on his three-mile walk the other day. He brought her back after less than a mile. She was walking slow and shaking at the hip. Arthritis and age have taken their toll. At thirteen years, she is not the blurred whirlwind of movement she was when, a decade ago, the woman left her with us for a one-week trial.

So, last night when I touched her lying beside the bed and listened to her snore, I felt and heard a warm presence of many years of deep love and company. It felt good and, knowing she was there, I slipped easily back into a sound sleep.

JENNIE
1981 – 2005

ABOUT THE AUTHOR

Paul Estronza La Violette has written several books about the life he and his wife, Stella, have led living on the beach of a small coastal town in Mississippi.

As a marine scientist, he sees the world of the coastal marsh and Mississippi Sound in a different way than many people. He talks about this in his books, interspersing stories of the people and the local way of life in the town. Anyone reading the books feels personally gratified, relating what they read to their own personal experiences.

Mr. La Violette lives on a beach road in Waveland, Mississippi, with Stella and a black tomcat named Holly.

ABOUT THE ARTIST

Patricia Rigney has illustrated three of my books and is a very dear friend. She is a native of Mississippi, born in Gulfport, Mississippi, and has spent much of her life on the Gulf Coast.

She received her formal training as an artist at William Carey College in Gulfport, graduating with a Bachelor's Degree in Fine Art in 1991.

She has had numerous shows, and selections of her work can be seen in the various art galleries along the Gulf Coast. At present, she lives in Waveland, Mississippi.